THE FATE OF AN EMPEROR

OVERLORD II

THE FATE OF AN EMPEROR

JD SMITH

TRISKELE BOOKS

The Fate of an Emperor copyright © 2014 JD Smith

The moral rights of the author have been asserted.

All rights reserved. No part of this publication may be reproduced, distributed, or transmitted in any form or by any means, including photocopying, recording, or other electronic or mechanical methods, without the prior written permission of the publisher, except in the case of brief quotations embodied in critical reviews and certain other non-commercial uses permitted by copyright law. For permission requests, write to the publisher, addressed "Attention: Permissions Coordinator," at the email address below.

Cover design and formatting www.jdsmith-design.com

Published by Quinn Publications

All enquiries to editor@quinnpublications.co.uk

First published 2014

ISBN Paperback: 978-0-9576164-5-5
ISBN Ebook: 978-0-9576164-6-2

For Ian on our tenth anniversary
(give or take a few months).

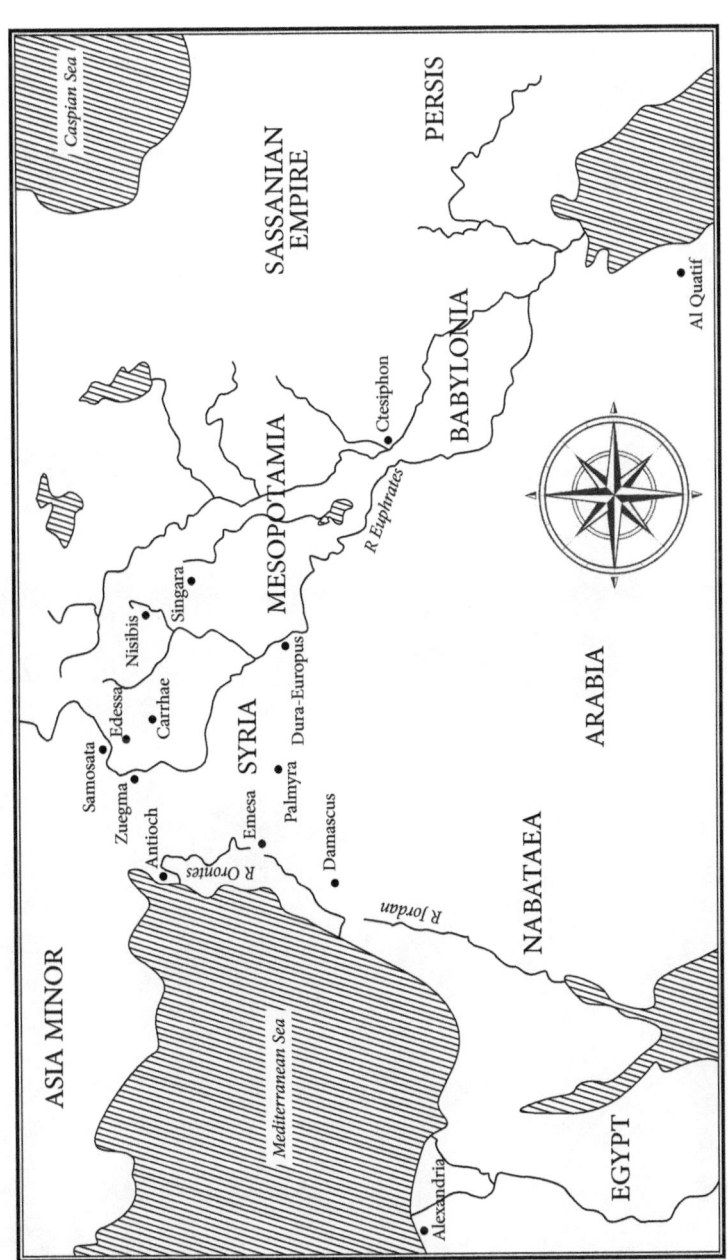

Roman East, 3rd Century AD

PROLOGUE

Zabdas – 258 AD

Sun cut through the small window, illuminating the room, cups and bowls, table, chairs, the blanket under which I lay entangled with Aurelia. I smoothed her pale gold hair as she looked at me, a smile of happiness that only the innocence of youth can buy touching her lips. And yet I knew different. Her slender fingers traced the fresh muscle on my unmarked chest, across my shoulders and down my arms to the only scar upon my body; a crude slave mark puckering the skin. She had known a life that on one hand saw the coldness of a father who would never love her and on the other the kindness of an old Roman senator who gave her the affection and education only a rare bastard-born could know.

'The gods know I am glad you came,' I said.

'Nowhere is safe,' she replied. 'Perhaps not even Palmyra now.'

It stung to hear those words, for another to think the capital of Syria, the city I loved and the centre of power on the Roman front could be at risk. I always thought it to be the one place immune to our enemy, impenetrable and safe, the heart of these lands.

'Palmyra is safe,' I murmured, more to myself than to her.

She moved closer, her head on my chest, arm around me, golden hair under my chin. I breathed in her scent, fresh and clean and of nothing more than the morning.

'Zenobia and Odenathus married under Roman law?' she said, a question and yet it was not the one spoken aloud. She knew the king and queen of Palmyra had breathed silent vows and signed a marriage contract in line with Roman custom.

'They did,' I said. 'And before they were bound by Roman law they were bound by their own Egyptian vows to one another, sharing a bed and the promise of fidelity and children to come. They will be faithful – as will we.'

I felt her nod against my chest and she said no more. I knew she worried and wondered whether or not we were truly man and wife if no Roman ceremony had been performed.

'Would you prefer it if we signed a Roman marriage contract?'

She was silent a moment, then said: 'We do not need to.'

'I am not a Roman, and my customs are not yours, Aurelia. I commit myself to you for now and for all time, to share your bed, to remain faithful only to you. But if it eases your mind to bind our marriage by the laws of your people, then we can do so.'

She did not reply. She kissed me instead, long and lingering. 'I do not need parchment to tell me what I know,' she breathed. 'If you consider me wife then that is enough.'

Banging sounded at the door.

'They are coming!' a voice shouted. 'They are coming!'

Fear rippled through me. Aurelia sat up, sheets pulled to her chest, hair hanging loose around her face, eyes wide.

'I must go,' I said.

'The Persians?'

I nodded.

'Stay safe.'

Safe? How could any of us stay safe? I felt a pang of frustration and annoyance at her coming here, to Antioch, washing away the past three nights that we had spent together behind the city walls.

You should not have come, I thought, but I dared not breathe

the words, could not show my fear and my anxiety to her. She had left the safety of Palmyra and come to the frontier for me so that we might have the life she had come to Syria to share. I could not resent her for that, but nor could I shake the dread that built and now threatened to erupt as the Persian enemy approached.

Harsh rapping sounded at the door.

'Move, move, move!'

I walked over to the door, opened it and looked out. Soldiers, half-armed, ran along the street. Terrified screams rang from the citizens.

I closed the door and turned to fetch my armour

'Are they already in the city?' Aurelia asked.

'I do not know. Bolt the door behind me. Open it for no one. If I do not return, head back to Palmyra and stay there. Do not endanger yourself.'

Something unnerved me. Before today there had been only a clash of wills, Valerian backing away from Shapur, enduring countless raids and harassment. But now we were under attack, trapped behind the walls of Antioch with nowhere to run.

Aurelia stood up and helped me fasten the straps of my breastplate. I turned and kissed her, those sweet lips, the faith and feeling of a woman upon them. Then I left, sword in hand.

Citizens ran in panic, prized possessions clutched in arms, frightened children dragged behind, cries and whimpers lingering in their wake. In the midst of chaos, units of soldiers marched through the streets. Orders sounded on all sides as Roman soldiers moved with purpose.

I picked up my pace, half-running along the street to the house where I knew Zenobia lived. Zenobia; now wife to the king of Palmyra and my half-sister. I could think only of her safety as I left Aurelia, knowing that Zenobia was not the same, she would not cower in the face of danger, would not hide behind a bolted door and stay there until my return. She would face the enemy head on as a soldier would, and I feared most that she would put herself in danger.

Against a dirty blue sky a rain of bright orange seared, humming through cold air and hammering down into the city. New screams coursed. I turned down one alleyway, then another, each one blocked by panic stricken people.

'Zabdas!'

I turned to see Zenobia struggling through the crowds, hands clutched to a swollen belly.

'I was coming for you. What are you doing out of the house?'

She did not hear me, or did not listen. Panting, she squeezed a path toward me.

'Have you seen Zabbai?' she asked.

'Not today.'

'Odenathus?'

I shook my head.

'Zenobia, it is my duty to ensure your safety. You must return to the house.'

Citizens shunted and pushed. I clutched her arm to steady her.

'The Persians breach our defences on the east side of the city. Odenathus was called from our bed not long ago. And our supply ships are being cut off.' She spoke like Zabbai or Odenathus or any other general, her words matter of fact, the din of the crowd penetrated by her authoritative voice.

My mind cleared of all thought as I realised that the city would begin to starve, blocked from our own lands by invaders.

I felt anger grip my heart as I thought of the man responsible, the Emperor who had travelled from Rome to bring aid, who had done nothing but hinder our defence, and I saw that anger reflected in Zenobia's eyes.

'What do you propose?' I said.

Her face hardened. 'I do not know.' She looked about her. 'I must find Zabbai and hope that he can persuade Odenathus to reclaim control over the army. Emperor Valerian cannot command. He has no notion of what is required of him. This

Zabdas - 258 AD

city will fall if Odenathus does not take charge.'

'It is not safe,' I replied. 'I will come with you.'

We pushed and squeezed a path through the streets, our pace hindered by those attempting to flee. Little did they know that no ships would see them safely downriver. Fires burned fierce, warming the seats of the gods – pleasing them, no doubt. What thoughts had they to torment for amusement at daybreak? How they must laugh as we mortals pushed and wrestled our way through a maze of stone and chaos.

We reached the east wall and found it twenty men deep, all armed, all ready to kill the Persians should they break through. Our enemy were adept on horseback, but now they were scaling the walls so skilfully I could almost have admired them if I had not felt the surge of panic and the desire to kill. Our own soldiers slashed and cut and poured hot oil from the tops of the walls, but the screams of the Persians were barely heard above the metal drum-beating coming from beyond the city, louder than the din of our soldiers, louder even than the pulsing of my heart in my ears. The sound brought fear, the kind that would see a man turn and run. And yet the men of Rome seemed to know this; they began their own chant to drown the sounds. Still I felt the chill of the Persian rhythm.

I clutched Zenobia's hand as we squeezed through the crowds looking for Zabbai, but he was not to be found. And before I realised it we were pushed through to where the soldiers stood before the gate barring the entrance to the city.

The emperor was nowhere in sight. On the walls I saw the enemy trying to gain control, screaming and wailing and disordered in contrast to the Roman soldiers.

'We should not be here,' I said to Zenobia, the thought of Odenathus' rage at his pregnant wife standing in the midst of soldiers defending the city turning my blood cold.

'They will break through,' she said.

'Which is why we must not be here when they do,' I retorted.

I looked over the heads of the soldiers. Behind the gates,

Roman soldiers prepared for the breach, the front row backing up two paces and levelling their spears.

'We must go. Zabbai is not here.' Panic edged my voice. I did not know what to do next. If the Persians broke through, only the twenty deep Romans stood between the enemy and the city. I tried to keep calm, to control my breathing and not let fear rise higher and higher.

I looked about me, spotted one of the king's generals, and moved across to him, pushing men from my path, pulling Zenobia with me. He gestured at the soldiers around him, waving his arms, attempting to bring order to the increasing chaos. I tried to remember his name. He was squat, unfriendly. It came to me.

'Pouja?' I shouted. 'Pouja?'

He took one glance at me and turned his back.

'Bastard,' I spat.

I glanced back at Zenobia, my grip on her wrist tightening, worried I'd lose her in the swarm of men.

'Fucking idiots!' Pouja bellowed.

He pushed through to the front of the group whose spear-tips pointed at the gate. It bulged inwards under the weight of the Persians.

My breath came fast and irregular. I could think of nothing for the dread that filled me, my legs weak as I tried to move but could not. I heard prayers muttered to numerous gods as the soldiers stood fast, holding their lines, eyes focussed. I glanced to either side, wondering how many men were as fearful as I, whether I would see my own fear reflected in their faces and polished shields.

Pouja stood to our left, his features grim yet showing an excitement I did not share. On my right a Roman warrior, his face expressionless, watched the gate. Someone pushed between us.

'Let's kill some of these bastards,' he screamed.

I looked into his wild eyes and returned a weak grimace.

The heavy armour of the Romans glinted in the moonlight. No, it was sunlight, hot and rising and for a fleeting, absurd moment I imagined how much hotter the Romans must be. They stood with one foot in front of the other, steady against the rush that would come, putting weight behind their tall shields that would protect us. I gripped my own shield, and felt suddenly vulnerable, naked.

'No!' Pouja cried.

A heartbeat later and the gate disintegrated in a mass of splintered wood and screeches and war-cries and the enemy swarmed toward us, thirsty for blood and for plunder. Kettle drums beat louder than before and I shivered and pushed down the urge to retch, and with fear and dismay I watched as time itself ground slower.

The call of the enemy came wild; a thunderous noise that filled my ears and reverberated around us. For a moment I was blinded by light reflected on shields. Screams of battle rang from Persian mouths. Their terrible war cries pierced my ears and the very heart of me feared what would come.

I could see no faces in the enemy ranks before they charged. Their heads were encased in metal helmets, their bodies a series of overlapping plates. On their legs they wore full-length boots, attached to their body armour and leaving no gap for our spears and swords. They were not on foot, but mounted on heavy, armoured horses.

Our front line dropped to their knees and lifted spears to adjust for the horses. They would aim below the beasts' breast plate, to injure and kill. But lances, longer and more substantial than our spears were levelled by the Persians, and they came at us and they hit our line with a force that crumpled the front rank into those behind, and beyond them in turn. Zenobia gripped my waist, steadying herself, and I cursed again and again that she had led us here, where the enemy pooled into the city.

Bloody carnage ensued. Horses trampled our soldiers and screams issued from our men as they fell beneath merciless hooves. I cried. Not in pain, but a great battle cry as I engaged the enemy, pulling from Zenobia's grip; a wolf on its prey.

'Barricade the gateway!' I heard someone shout. But it was impossible. What remained of the gates hung limp as the Persian knights pushed through, forcing us back. I realised it must have been Pouja shouting, for the command was in Syrian. Then I heard more shouts. '*Barricade porta*,' came the command in Latin.

The wild-eyed Syrian next to me pushed his way through the press of men and drove a short sword into the flank of an enemy horse. The beast reared and wailed, throwing its rider to the ground, where Roman soldiers drove their swords home.

Sun flashed in my vision. My ears filled with cries and shouts and clanging. I could not distinguish my own voice. It was as if I made no sound. I tried to move my sword, but we were too tightly packed. A faceless enemy came toward me, but I could only scratch his armour. I was terrified, my bladder constricting and sweat pouring. He turned his horse and rounded on me. I could not think, did not know what to do. It would be death by blade or crushed by heavy horse and seen from this world.

With all of my strength I pulled my sword hand free and arced the bright steel, grabbing the bottom edge of the Persian bastard's breastplate in my left, throwing all my weight to pull him from his horse. He toppled, the weight of his armour forcing him to the ground with a crash. Rider-less, his horse reared, confused.

Then I killed for the first time.

He was sprawled on the floor. I hesitated. The sword in my hand felt suddenly limp.

The Syrian beside hollered: 'Lift his helmet and slit his throat.'

I glanced down, still hesitating, as more Persian warriors flooded through the gate. We were being overwhelmed.

'Kill the bastard,' the Syrian shouted again.

My hands shook. My grip slipped with sweat. I breathed deeply, knowing what must be done. I bent down, lifted the chin of the Persian's helmet. He struggled, but he could not move, even if I had not held my sword to his throat and my knee in his chest. And with one, quick movement, I dragged my blade across his exposed throat and watched his blood spurting onto the ground.

It took a heartbeat to comprehend what I had done.

The world became a different place, where warriors kill or let themselves be killed, and children learn to be men or die.

My whole body wavered with shock. I could barely stand, but then a feeling, strong and frightening, ran through me. I stepped over the man I had just sent to the Otherworld and I killed again and again. Now *I* was covered in the blood of the enemy. I had eyes and ears only for death. It was my duty to my country, to the people of Syria, and to Zenobia, the girl with whom I had travelled to Rome in order to secure an army large enough to defeat the enemy. And I had no idea where she was.

Bloody scratches, grazes and streaks of sweat hatched my skin, but I felt no pain. I was so absorbed in combat that I did not realise we had forced the Persians back through the gateway. Bodies were moved out of the way and what remained of the gates were swung closed.

'Out of the way,' voices bellowed

Timber was brought forward to reinforce our defence, hastily put across the gate, then more butted up to it.

I cut down one last man with a satisfying blow. I looked about me. The fallen bled and cried and begged for aid or lay lifeless. Two screeching horses were put out of their misery; I felt the waste. Soldiers looked to each other, relieved, smiling even, at their survival.

Then the force of the moment before hit me. My limbs trembled uncontrollably. I gasped for breath. Cuts stung and I almost dropped to my knees.

'You feel most alive in the moments before you're about to die,' a voice said.

I did not reply, but gripped my knees with my hands.

'You've never killed a man?' the Syrian said, gripping my elbow in support.

He looked at me as though he knew me. I suppose he did. We had fought together, side by side. We were brothers now, comrades in battle.

'No,' I said, embarrassment stealing my strength.

'You can tell. Scared of the need. Unsure how to finish it.'

I nodded.

'You'll come to know it. Once you start, there is no changing what you have done, that you've taken another life. That you enjoyed it.'

CHAPTER I

Zabdas – 258 AD

Zabbai appeared beside me, caught my shoulder, looked down at the men I had killed.

'A soldier now, boy.'

I peered at the lifeless bodies, bloody and still, not quite knowing what to think as the city buzzed around me.

'You do well, lad, you do well.'

He patted my shoulder but he was looking about us, assessing the damage, surveying the scene of carnage before him.

I looked behind me for sign of Zenobia and saw King Odenathus, his height offering him a good hand above many of the soldiers. Full armour hung from his solid frame. Confusion and anger lined his face.

'Pouja, to me!' he called over the crowds. 'We must organise this defence. Zabbai, move more reinforcements behind this gate. Get archers on the damned wall up there and make sure the bastard scum are stuck with feathers if they come anywhere near us. We need to organise this fucking chaos.'

Zenobia moved beside him and my gaze flickered to her. Her eyes raked the scene of blood and death and dying horses. Odenathus saw me and followed my line of sight. His face displeased, impatient, tired even, but I could see little anger in his features, only resignation. Odenathus turned back to face the walls. Zabbai was already securing a garrison behind the gate and archers were spreading out along the wall above.

'Pouja?' the king called again.

'My lord?' the general replied, pushing through the mass. Breathless and blood-streaked, sweat poured from his face.

'It appears they are falling back. I want to get on the walls. We need to assess the situation more fully. I do not trust what is happening and we are on our own in this; the Romans concentrate their main force to the south of the city.'

'You have spoken with Emperor Valerian?' Zenobia said.

Odenathus grunted confirmation.

'Why can you not do as I ask, Zenobia? Why is it so difficult for you to simply obey?' When she did not reply he said to me, 'You should never have let her out of the damned house.'

Even as he spoke I saw the regret on his face. He knew I had not been posted at their house that morning, and even if I had been I could not have stopped her.

Shaking from the enemy encounter I stumbled through the crowds, brushing shoulders with soldiers, my mind reeling but at the same time clear as to our need to protect the city. Behind us, in the heart of the city, citizens cried and screamed. They would be running to the temples to give prayers to the gods, or burying what they could not carry from the city. It had not fallen yet, but the Persians had breached this gate, and I dreaded to think how many others.

High up on the walls hundreds of archers now swarmed, their bows trained outwards. We climbed the steps, Odenathus, Zabbai, Zenobia and I. The din of the enemy beyond grew louder the higher we climbed.

At the top, stood high on the city wall, we paused a few feet from the edge and I saw then the force we faced. On all sides we were swamped so deep in a sea of men that no land appeared beyond the crawling mass of Persian warriors. We were perhaps thirty feet up; high enough to see a hundred thousand men on foot and horse. Chariots glimmered in a hazy sun, and far beyond sat the palisade upon which King Shapur would watch his army wage war on our land. Never in my life had I seen so many men.

'The emperor,' Zabbai said.

I looked behind me, down into the city where the soldiers parted as Emperor Valerian strode toward the wall, his purple robe dragging through the dust.

'Odenathus,' he called up, 'you requested my presence?'

'This wall was moments ago breached. It is secure enough now. Come up.'

'You would see us put on display to the enemy, so that they can pick us from the walls with their arrows, Lord King?' Sarcasm mingled with fear laced the title with which Valerian addressed Odenathus.

'No, Caesar. I merely show you the enemy we face. There is nothing to fear, they have moved out of range of our bowmen, so we are not within range of theirs.' Odenathus swept his arm, encompassing the army before us. His voice was cool as midday heat crept upon us. His words may have been humorous, but his aged eyes and stern face echoed the seriousness of our situation.

Valerian climbed the steps, hesitated, then neared the edge of the wall for a view of the lands beyond our sanctuary. Colour drained from his cheeks as surely as a drunk would drain a cup of wine. At the sight of his purple cloak, the noise of the Persian kettle drums heightened, the noise itself enough to put fear into the gods themselves.

'Ignore it,' Zabbai said to me. 'They intend to make you fear them, do not let them succeed.'

But they did. I felt it penetrate me the same way the heat makes you sweat; you cannot stop.

I fixed my expression, my cold face, for I was a soldier; a warrior of the east. I would not show fear just as Zabbai showed nothing, and Odenathus spoke without emotion to the emperor. We could not let ourselves be overcome. Warrior hearts must beat in our breasts. If we were to die, then it must be in battle: a soldiers' death.

'We must not attempt to face them again in head on combat,' Odenathus said. 'The Persians know they outnumber us. Our priority must be to keep the city safe, to guard the walls against penetration and alleviate the blockage of our supply ships on the river.'

Valerian opened his mouth, as if to argue. He backed from the wall, as far as he could without retreating down the steps, back into the city.

'We will be starved within the confines of the walls!'

Odenathus shook his head.

'There is enough food for ten, perhaps twelve weeks. In that time we must concentrate our efforts on re-establishing the supplies. This city is a fortress. The Persians will tire and when they move on to other lands, we will be ready to take them, ready to move.'

'We will punish them for what they have done,' Zenobia said.

'You think I do not want to punish them?' Valerian asked.

Zenobia looked at him as if a child pulled at the edge of her gown.

'I am in command here, Odenathus,' Valerian said, turning. 'Not you. You may have loyalty from your countrymen, but this is my army.'

Odenathus' eyes narrowed, and he paused.

'Of course, Caesar. I did not question your authority.'

Valerian lowered his voice. They talked, words only for one another's ears. Then Odenathus nodded and Valerian turned and retreated back down and into the city.

Beyond the wall, the enemy pounded on their shields and drums and roared obscenities, the absence of the emperor from the walls a victory in itself.

Odenathus steadied his gaze on the amassing army. Zenobia moved to his side, their shoulders almost touching, her belly swollen and hard and the unity they had formed evident as they stood at ease with one another. Jealousy seared, the knowledge that they were now irrevocably tied to one another tightening my throat, foaming in my stomach. She was my half-sister, and I wondered daily if my love for her was just that of a sibling, having never known such love before now, but I could never shake my desire and my continual thoughts of her. She was even more beautiful with a child in her belly, the roundness of it, the glow in her cheeks, the warmth. Her eyes were slicked with kohl and I knew I would never be capable of looking deep enough into those windows to know her completely.

'Odenathus,' Zabbai said, shaking me from thought.

The king peered across at us; one man his friend, the other a boy of whom he knew so little and cared even less. I was a friend, half-brother and guard to Zenobia, our mother one and the same, her father as good as mine, but to Odenathus I was nothing more than the sum of my functions. Every time he looked at me, it was as if it were the first time, a new face in his company, a distant stranger whose name was not worth remembering. After all the time I had spent in his presence, even now he looked past me.

'I doubt they will assault the walls again today. This was a warning, that they are here and in force,' Odenathus mused.

'They will starve us into surrender,' Zabbai said.

'They will not,' Zenobia replied.

Odenathus continued to look upon the enemy as if none of us had spoken.

Clouds moved above. The gateway that had been a tangle of warriors killing and screaming was now quiet. The dead had been taken and tended, the surviving enemy inside our walls killed.

As we stood there in silence, the enemies' shouting and drum-beats ceased. Did they contemplate returning to camp? Perhaps. The afternoon wore on and the cold of night would soon be upon us. I thought of the Persians and of the first man I had killed, the wildness of his eyes. He was a man, but I could not think of him as being the same. They were inhuman to me, yet I knew they were people, just like us, with homes and farms and families waiting for their return. Waiting for the plunder they would bring. Was the plunder they would gain from raiding our country necessary for them to survive? I thought not.

Syrians shouted abuse over the walls, that Shapur's mother was impregnated by pigs when she conceived him. That his father, Ardashir, could father nothing.

'If they do not attack, I will rest,' Zenobia said.

'Of course,' Odenathus replied, and I thought perhaps he was relieved at that.

I moved to escort her, but the king caught my arm and gestured below for another soldier to go with her.

'My lord, what troubles you?' I asked.

Clouds descended over the hills to the north; a bad omen. We prized water, but this was no time for the gods' wrath.

Once Zenobia was out of sight, Odenathus said, 'Does Zenobia speak to you of Rome?'

'In what way?'

He paused, as if unsure whether or not to trust me.

'I am uneasy,' he confessed. 'Does she wish to sever Syria from Rome, as her father does, or will she seek the aid of the Romans in our efforts to purge Syria of our enemies?'

'Both,' Zabbai said.

'I am certain, my Lord,' I said, 'that Zenobia is as true to you and Palmyra as she is to her father. It was Julius' wish that Palmyra be free of invasion. She is close to him, and she endeavours to please him. But she is your wife, in the eyes of both Syria and Rome.' I could have bitten my tongue as I spoke, the words feeling bitter in my mouth. To speak of their marriage. 'She does only what is best,' I finished, knowing that I had given no real answer, that I did not have one. Zenobia did as she wished.

Odenathus let out a long, slow breath. He reminded me of someone tormented, his face so full of thought it pained him to attempt concentration on a single matter for longer than a moment.

'You are her friend and her half-brother,' he said, brushing my comment aside. 'You have said what I expected you to say.'

'My Lord, you know Julius well. You are friends. If you trust him, then you can trust her. Zenobia and her father are one. They strive to achieve the same goals. She does only what she feels will secure both your command in the east and the safety of your people. She knows that you cannot scourge these lands without more men. It is why she journeyed to Rome. You owe her much.'

'Zabdas is right,' Zabbai said. 'She may share her father's hopes, but she is not foolish. She does what is necessary for the safety of Syria. You can be sure of that.'

Odenathus gave a curt nod.

'Zabbai, organise the men,' he said. 'Set a night watch in place. Our soldiers are to be ready for battle at a moment's notice.'

Zabbai faltered.

'Go.'

Odenathus was tall; much taller than me. Bedouin leather stretched across his chest, bare arms glinted with sweat in a dying light.

'I know that you do not like me,' he said, and began to pace along the wall.

'My Lord …'

'No, Zabdas,' he said, and raised a hand. 'As your king, you are not required to like me. It was not my decision to keep you from the Euphrates.' He spoke gravely.

My heart lurched into my throat and my stomach churned. Did he know? Were my tormented feelings plain upon my face? I could not bring myself to like Odenathus. I had known that ever since he had sent Julius south, away from me, to wage war on the southern tribes. Ever since he had taken Zenobia as his wife because, gods damn it, despite my being her half-brother I could not banish my own affections. Feelings that were more than that of a brother.

'Julius *is* my friend,' Odenathus said. 'He does not want harm to come to you.'

His words carried a warning, that my involvement in Zenobia's wellbeing was unwanted. What would he do if I kept my proximity? I waited, my mouth drier than the desert.

'Go back to your woman,' he said, 'and get some rest. The coming weeks will be long.'

I turned, relief sudden and welcome and warm. Then a thought came to mind.

'When they attack, I wish to fight.' I had trained as a soldier, yet until today I had not participated in full-on combat. I was young and reckless. I dreamt of becoming a warrior, and of the profits and glory that came with it. And despite Julius not wanting me to join him in the south, perhaps I might now be permitted to fight alongside my brothers.

'Like you did today?' Odenathus asked, looking down at my tunic and the Persian blood crusting upon my breast. Grazes, red and angry on my arms, stung. 'It is not always as easy as it was today. War is no fun for those who die.'

I nodded and took my leave, knowing I was dismissed.

I pondered Odenathus' last words as the sun disappeared and the city streets were cast in shadow. Soldiers lay restless in their beds or guarded the walls, citizens hid in their homes, knowing that they must feed and billet soldiers for months. All was quiet as I returned to the house where I hoped Aurelia waited, out of danger, more obedient than Zenobia could ever be.

I walked in solitude. Not one Roman I had met appreciated the glory of the eastern cities, thinking their own mighty Rome superior. Intricate mosaics and polished marble were trodden on without a second thought, and all the while I looked on, embittered by their lack of respect, protective of that which I felt a part of.

The guards outside our house nodded and let me pass. All was quiet, the modest rooms empty, everyone retired to their beds. I found Aurelia waiting for me, fully dressed in the silks so prized in the Italian markets. She greeted me with a smile that said we needed to talk. She poured wine, handed it to me and took one for herself, before beckoning me to sit with her.

Only now did I realise, as I sipped the wine and sat down for the first time that day, how tired I was, in body and mind. Aurelia, her sweet young face unlined, unscarred, unhindered by age, stared at me.

She touched a jewelled hand on mine, licked a finger of her other hand and wiped my cheek. My anger drained away. Life sifted, calm left behind.

'You fought today, Zabdas,' she said, indicating the blood she wiped from my face.

'I did,' I murmured, intoxicated by the perfumes enhancing her soft, pale skin, not paying attention to what she said, not really caring. My ears turned her words into sweet music, every breath a new song.

'You killed men?'

'A few.'

She kissed me where the blood had been, as if it would cleanse the action of taking life. I had protected the city. She understood that, I was sure, but did she fear for my soul, for what the gods would do?

'Do not turn into my father, Zabdas.' She paused, looked into my eyes, focussing on one then the other. 'He is a cruel man, without a heart and with a soul so fragmented by all the lives he has taken. To kill in defence is acceptable, and my father does, but they say he takes enjoyment, that he shares the sport of the gods. I beg you, do not be the same.'

She kissed my lips.

'Cor meum cum corde tuo usque in sempiternum.'

My heart is yours forever.

Her murmured words hung on the evening air, refusing to fade.

I trembled as I held her, shoulders aching beneath the weight of day. She shared that weight by being with me, being close, not realising how much I needed her touch and the sound of her soft voice in my ear.

Guilt pierced the calm. I had not thought of her as I faced the enemy, not as I killed nor as I worried for Zenobia. I cursed myself for a fool.

Then I felt ashamed. I should not have felt guilt; guilt was for the weak. They say emotion makes you more of a man, more real, more alive, that you see life in fair perspective and you can overcome your inner demons with reason. But I should not have felt this emotion. I should only experience anger and controlled rage, for when I took the life of a Persian, I became more than just a man.

I was a soldier; a warrior of the east.

CHAPTER 2

Samira – 290 AD (Present day)

I CANNOT IMAGINE MY grandfather as a young man, taking the life of a Persian in all the heat and sweat and dread of battle. I am afraid, I think, to hear that he might fall to a sword or spear, even though he could not, for if he had I would not be looking at him this moment as he stares back upriver.

His face is aging and I notice with each passing day the new lines upon his face and the marks cut into his flesh that were not there before. He is my only family, the single living person bound to me by blood, now my own father is gone.

Vaballathus.

I say his name over and again and it rides in my mind as I drift on this boat. I have not stopped thinking of him since his death, since the moment my grandfather told me of his being cut down by the king of the Tanukh, the man they called Jadhima.

The laughter I hear from my grandfather's men, the men whose boat this is, reminds me of my father, of the way he always laughed and joked and made light of the world, of a country in the wake of war.

My grandfather will not speak of his death and I know that my father brought it upon himself, that he would not listen, took his own path, brought danger upon himself and others. It was always his way. I see him clearly, thinking himself right, stubborn and younger than his years. I am unsure who the child is, my grandfather would say.

We anchor at Arethusa and go ashore, the ground unsteady beneath my feet. We are to buy provisions to last until Hama, and from there I do not know. Rostram owns the boat upon which we travel, a slave trader and a pirate, a man my grandfather knows from long ago, the man who saved us from ransom, who took the lives of a boat's crew. And I do not think the man would see us much further, indeed he will not have to. Soon this river will peter out, a stream only, not fit to see a boat much further north.

'You look tired, grandfather,' I say, as we walk the streets of Arethusa.

He draws in a deep breath, and winces as if it pains him.

'Not as tired as I was. The death of Jadhima has lifted a heavy weight I have born for many years. I feel much lighter now.'

He lies, I think, for I know he feels no lightness, not with Jadhima's death weighted by my father's. I see grandfather's face begin to sag and his shoulders droop a little as if indeed he no longer has a weight to bear.

'You killed for the first time at the gates of Antioch,' I say. The death of the slavers on the river by my grandfather's hand comes to mind, the bloody decks and screams that I cannot forget. They haunt me at night, the first cries of death I have known. I cannot help but think of Palmyra and the death of Jadhima, parted from this world by my grandfather's sword.

'I did,' he replies, mouth curving into a smile at the memory. 'I became a soldier that day. My youth left me. I was responsible for my actions and I did not regret them.'

'You are proud?' I ask, and I can hear my own scorn.

'I protected the city, my people and my friends. I am proud of that.'

'But you killed?' I understand the necessity but not the joy.

'You said you felt incredible guilt, but you do not feel it now?'

'Not now. In time I discovered there is only one way to stand against an enemy. You cannot be cowed into silence. Roar the battle cry of the people or stand and liberate with words.'

'Why did Valerian lead the Roman army east, instead of his son Gallienus?' I ask. 'It was Gallienus who agreed that the east required aid.'

'I do not know. Perhaps Valerian wanted to keep Gallienus from Zenobia; it was obvious to many that he was attracted to her, that he spoke against his father and co-emperor because of her. It was also true that the pair had long agreed to split the Empire: Gallienus taking the west; Valerian the east.'

I think of Valerian, the emperor who retreated from the Persians, who backed his army to Antioch and hid behind its walls, a coward.

'I do not understand why Odenathus did not take command over his men.'

'Odenathus was a proud man who fought his conscience over many things, but none so much as his choice to follow the Roman line. Loyalty was his one weakness. That much I learned. He had long been faithful to Rome, but always in his mind were Julius' words. He did not know whether it would be better for his people if Syria declared itself independent, set itself aside, became an empire in its own right and thus give him imperium, or stay with Rome and never know.'

'Would it have been, at that time?'

Grandfather pauses. 'It is hard to say. I knew and respected Julius and his wishes for the east, but did not think until much later whether what he wanted would have been achievable. We needed Rome and its army, but under another general.'

I smile at the stall-holders, the merchants and boys running back and forth on errands. The slaves. Back home in Tripolis there were many, but not in our household, and I look at my grandfather's arm and the leather binding it and I think of the slave-mark which hides beneath, the past he has told me of and the years he spent in slavery. And I know too that he looks at these children in the market, and he tries not to supress the desire to buy them all and take them away, for he knows he cannot. Many are not for sale, and those who might be he cannot protect.

We exchange coin for figs and dates and peaches, for loaves of bread and barrels of beer. My grandfather's men help carry them back to the dock, to the boat, to load them aboard so we might continue upon our journey, to a place I have long wished to visit, to deliver the news of Jadhima's fate. We travel now to Rome. An excitement stirs inside me and I know a smile is creeping across my face, wide and without restraint. Grandfather does not notice. He is in his own world, one of the past, not the present, thinking no doubt upon the next portion of his tale, and what happened to Antioch.

CHAPTER 3

Zabdas – 258 AD

I woke to Aurelia's intoxicating presence. Her scent hung in the fresh morning hours, musty and tempting, as she stroked my arm, fingers passing across a sword scratch from the day before. I pulled her closer and she kissed my chest, her moist breath warming my skin. I slid my fingers through her soft hair.

Shouts from the household disturbed us, our billeting unwelcome despite my insistence that we took the smallest room, dark and cramped.

I groaned and rolled onto my back.

'I must go to Zenobia,' I said, not wanting to leave my bed and the press of Aurelia's pale nakedness on my own, darker flesh. I had not slept well in months, our low black tents unkind and unyielding in the open, but now, in a cot with Aurelia, I could sleep on through the mornings and into the afternoon if the gods would allow.

In silence she slid from the straw mattress. She pulled on silk robes, her hair tousled and long down her back, the fresh morning tightening the skin of her legs. She looked over her shoulder and smiled, sad and sweet and thoughtful.

The guard and I accompanied Zenobia through the streets. The Romans had already begun to train and I watched with curiosity as they lined in formations, each man deep in concentration, as if in their own private battle, toned muscle dark with the sun.

The Palmyrene army gathered to the east of the city, near the walls. It was there Zenobia joined Odenathus.

'You will accompany me today, Zenobia,' he said.

She nodded. I suspected the king simply wished her to stay where he could watch her, but she appeared content.

To us he said: 'Go to Pouja. He will give you orders for the day.'

We strolled further along the wall, past drying puddles of blood from the day before, to where Pouja relieved the night watch and designated a new one. He gave us orders to join the new watch.

I climbed up onto the city wall and with apprehension at what I might see, looked first left then right, down the length of wall. From there I could see the guard change around the perimeter of the city, men from different countries spread out, surrounding all we had fought to protect, facing the same foe. I looking directly out, afraid I would find the enemy a hand's breadth from my face, but it was not. The Persian force seemed much larger than it had the previous day, though they were still beyond the range of our archers. Their silks tunics might allow them to pull arrows clean from a wound, but they were unwilling to risk the whistle of death.

Mid-morning came and the enemy began to shift. Pouja shouted for the king to be fetched, and Odenathus arrived within moments, up and onto the wall with us. Beside him, Zabbai shielded his gaze. Both men's eyes were dark and sunken, both men lost in the need to hold the city, knowing that if we did not, that if we let Antioch fall … They spoke for a few moments more, then Odenathus disappeared back down the ladder, back to the ground to speak with the Roman generals.

Zabbai said to me: 'They are going to attack again.'

'Are we not starving anyway? I thought they intended to wait for us to hand over the city?'

'So we thought.'

'What then?'

'Something stirs in their camp.'

Zabbai worried me, the uncertainty in his voice. I had come to know him since we had returned together from Rome. My closeness to Zenobia, leading her personal guard, and his friendship with the king, we saw much more of one another.

'Odenathus has gone to warn the emperor and alert the Roman army. We have managed to gain a little more control over our own men, and with Odenathus a leader again, we will be ready for them this time.'

Zabbai's admiration for Odenathus' leadership qualities bit, but I could not deny even to myself that I felt safer, more assured, facing the enemy with the king in command.

The armies of Rome and Syria assembled behind the walls, the streets below the heavily defended parapets heaving with iron. I braced myself for the attack, the Persians edging nearer, my desperation at the need to stay alive growing stronger, to ensure that Zenobia's child made safe passage into the word. My grip on my sword tightened.

The soldiers backed away from the walls and archers took their place. I could no longer see the Persians. All along the perimeter legionaries banked deep in defence. We had the advantage. And we would keep it if no ill decisions were made. Even with the river blocked, we had weeks, months even, of supplies within the city. The enemy must have known. They were not prepared to wait. Their men were tireless for plunder, and Antioch could provide greater wealth than any city they had taken thus far.

Shouts and screams sounded from outside the city. Around me, grim-faced soldiers readied themselves for the assault, praying to the gods, tightening the straps of their armour, muttering unheard words to wives. I wished I had said more to Aurelia. I realised suddenly how little I had said to her, how many times she told me she loved me, and how little I had returned those words. I will change that, I swore, if I live.

'It is a good day to die.'

To my right, the wild-eyed Syrian grinned. He looked to the sky. An eagle flew overhead, wings blocking the sun for a heartbeat.

With little joy I smiled back. A good day. Was it? To me it was a day like any other of late, of death and fighting and the never ending prospect that this would continue until my last day. That it would never be done. Julius had wanted to free himself from Rome, and Zenobia wanted the same, but I could not see it. It would make no difference. I would still know blood and death, victory and defeat. Death crossed my mind, as it had before, but I could not accept it as the Syrian did now. His eyes bore into me as if he knew I harboured fear. He was older than me, but not by much. An understanding expression crossed his face and he looked back beyond walls where drums beat their fearful noise and roused dread in our people.

With no orders to the contrary, we waited.

'Let them come,' the Syrian shouted. 'Let them come so we can rip their rotting bowels from them to feed our dogs.' A cheer from our men deafened me.

'We will rip the heads from your shoulders and shit down your necks!'

Filled with excited fear, I too shouted the obscenities I heard others cry, releasing the tension I felt within.

Eventually, our throats dry and our spirits waning, we fell silent. Not a single archer had released an arrow as the enemy hung back, out of range.

And we waited.

Drums beat a rhythmic sound.

Valerian came within sight of the troops, Odenathus with him. They talked, mouths moving rapidly, the king pulling a hand through his beard as he spoke. Their horses stepped impatiently and as they parted I glimpsed Zenobia. Mounted beside her husband, amidst the dirty soldiers, the sweating horses, the stench of leather and men, she shone as a goddess would. Thick hair hung in a heavy braid, circlets of gold upon her forehead, around her throat, crossing over her breasts, with a light white gown skimming the unborn. Her love for the east was known by many, and beneath the expression of stone, she would be desperate to dictate what should be done.

Odenathus spoke urgently. Valerian bridled, lips curling, arms raised, face flushed with annoyance.

Eventually they turned their mounts and the generals of Rome and Stratego of the east moved through the army to take command. Odenathus nodded to Zenobia. Whatever thoughts stirred in her mind had been put to Valerian. It was for him to decide our fate.

Soon we would know it.

Impatient, I said, 'The Persians are waiting.'

'They'll come,' the Syrian replied. 'You know you're alive when you fight.'

We were of similar height, his expression like the mountain winds, with no real purpose except enjoyment. In one hand he held a spear, the point sharp and the shaft long. On his other arm he bore a shield, round and neat, and his wrists were bound with leather. Above the leather scars of more than just battle, of a scrape of stone, of a slipped chisel, marked his skin. He was a worker; a master of labours.

'What is your name?' he asked.

'Zabdas.'

I swayed in the heat. We waited for an enemy that would not come, an enemy who wanted to plunder and retreat, leaving the land desolate. I had nothing to say. If I spoke of the enemy I felt the fear rise, so I swallowed it, forcing myself to think other thoughts, of days hunting, riding, reed-lined waters, not daring to contemplate what would become of us.

'Where are you from, Zabdas?' he asked.

'Yemen,' I said, my anticipation fading with distraction and the images I had begun to conjure with it. 'And you?'

'My home is Antioch.'

'Then do you fight for the king and for Syria, or for your home and your family?'

The question did not need asking. It matter not what this Syrian fought for, but I was intrigued by him, his easy grin, his carefree expression, that the other soldiers did not have.

Beyond the walls, the cry of battle filled the sky.

'I fight for myself.' He shrugged. 'And you, my little friend, what do you fight for? A dream? A vision you cannot rid yourself of? Your own family?'

I thought of the mother and father I had been ripped from, of Julius in the south, the man who had found me, saved me, taken me into his home, and of Meskenit, Julius' wife and my true mother. Gods, I must bridge the years we had been parted, no matter the hurt she felt and the memories I knew she harboured, of a Roman penetrating her against her will, and me, the boy born of that act.

'I fight for my family and Syria,' I said. 'And I fight for my king.' The last words left me as easily as I felt fear in the face of the enemy. I fought for Zenobia, for her will and what she wanted to achieve, knowing that everything she did was to protect Palmyra. And if I fought for the safety of Palmyra then I fought for the king, despite my hatred of the man who had sent Julius to fight the Tanukh. And I fought for Aurelia; my lover and my friend.

'And you, friend of Antioch, what is your name?' I asked.

'Bamdad,' he replied with a grin.

Orders relayed back and forth. We waited for the archers to fire the first round of volleys. We would know then that the enemy were closing in. But the release of iron-tipped death never came. The archers' arms relaxed.

We waited all day, the sun's heat rippling the air, and my thoughts turned to the Persians and how they must be baking in the iron armour encasing their bodies. My lips were dry and I was thankful when water-skins were passed between the crush of soldiers. Even Bamdad, who had been maniacally gleeful at the thought of battle, became more subdued, his face falling into a frown and his eyes thoughtful.

Eventually, our watch released and a new one in place, we headed for bed.

'You enjoy dice?' Bamdad asked me.

'I do.'

'I know a few places in the city where the stakes are not so high, the drink cheap, and the women cheaper,' he said.

I thought of Aurelia alone, worried, waiting for my return.

'I have to get back.'

'Your loss, my friend. If you change your mind I'll be in the northern quarter.' He winked and left.

I strolled back to the house where Aurelia would be. The city seemed quiet once more. I began unbuckling my armour and entered the house.

Zenobia stood before me, pale face stern with worry.

'What is wrong?' I asked.

'The city's water supply has been poisoned.'

'What, all of it?'

'Almost every source. The wells outside the city and those inside too.'

'Then the Persians have men inside the walls?'

'Perhaps. They may well be inside the city, or they have the sympathies of men of Antioch.'

'What does the emperor or Odenathus do?'

'They have cut off all supplies to stop sickness. Odenathus has sent men to look for whoever might have been responsible, but I do not hold much hope, they are likely too discreet or long gone.'

I thought for a moment. 'I met a man of Antioch today. Perhaps he has heard murmurs of discontent. He might know something.'

In the dark and noisy northern quarter we found Bamdad. He sat in a tavern, a whore on the bench next to him, her arm wrapped lazily around his shoulder, her lips pursed in promise.

He caught my eyes and laughed.

'You join me then?'

I shook my head as Zenobia lifted back her hood. Bamdad looked curiously between the two of us, a smile still on his face.

'My cousin,' I said.

'The queen?' Bamdad replied.

'And her personal guard.'

He nodded. 'Then I take it you're not here for the women and the dice?' he said.

'No, my friend.'

Bamdad sighed and lifted the whore's arm from his neck. She stood up and left, a curt glance at us for our intrusion.

Zenobia sat down beside Bamdad and I sat opposite.

'The water supplies in the city have been poisoned. Zabdas tells me you are a local, and therefore you might have information. Knowledge of someone within the city who could side with the Persians?'

'I have a wife and three children in this city,' he replied. Fret and worry simmered beneath the surface of the Syrian, shattering his joyful humour. If the city fell … He and his family, if they survived, would become slaves; playthings of our enemy. He was a husband, a father and a warrior, but he was also a man of Antioch. He knew the city better than anyone.

'Do you know anything which might tell us who has betrayed Antioch?' Zenobia asked.

Bamdad's face creased. 'It was you who meddled in the conviction of the senator Mareades.'

'It was. Tell me, do you know who might have done this? Or how the Persians might have infiltrated the city? They cannot have done it alone.'

'There are some who know the truth,' Bamdad said, ignoring her words, his own voice little more than a whisper.

'The truth?' Zenobia asked.

'Yes. Many of us believe the priest Haddudan, who convicted Mareades, who swore the senator's guilt, is a liar and a thief.'

'It is true,' I said. 'The priest king is the man who stole from you and the people of Antioch. And yet we could do nothing. Mareades would have been dead before Haddudan was brought to trial. We did what we could for him.'

'The priest covered his tracks?' Bamdad said.

'We are wasting time,' Zenobia reminded us.

Bamdad's eyes flickered between the two of us and he leaned closer. 'There is another way into the city.'

'The gate to the east is manned by Roman soldiers,' Zenobia said. 'The emperor posted them himself. They monitor every person, every cart going in and out of the city.'

Bamdad shook his head. 'Not on the east side. There is another entrance. Concealed. To the north. Few know of its existence.'

'You think that could be their way in?' I asked, my voice lower still, aware of ears in the room.

'Perhaps,' Zenobia replied. 'Show me this path into the city. If it is not already manned, then it should be.'

We pushed our way through the streets, citizens about their market trade despite the lack of water, the heat of day, the enemy beyond the walls ... I could see the fear in their faces, the fact that they were close to crumbling, and I wanted to reach out to them, to reassure, but in my own heart I felt the same fear, rooted in the knowledge that one or more of the people within these very walls had betrayed us.

'Why did no one tell the king or the emperor of this other entrance?' Zenobia asked. 'The lives of the people in this city depend on the city walls, the safety they afford.'

Bamdad glanced this way and that, threading a path, leading us on.

'Few know of its existence, fewer still that it is still an open passage. It is well hidden. A smugglers' entrance,' he continued.

'Opened ten years or more after it was first blocked. The guards are paid by merchants who have goods couriered in and out of the city.'

'How do you know of it?' I asked.

'I have worked for the less honest in my time,' he replied.

We broke into less crowded streets. Zenobia bent forward, her breathing heavy.

'Wait,' I shouted to Bamdad.

'We keep going,' she said. 'Which way now?'

Bamdad pointed to our right, a narrow street, tall buildings casting shadows.

Our footsteps echoed as we followed.

'Do you trust him?' Zenobia asked me, her voice low.

'I barely know him. We fought together at the gate, nothing more.'

We crossed into another street, then another, past women washing clothes and old men throwing dice. Boys crowded around wells, peering down at the poisoned water as horses drank from troughs.

'This way,' Bamdad said.

He led us to a building with bowing walls. A door hung on rusted hinges. Zenobia and I shared a sceptical glance as the Syrian lifted the door's latch. With a dull squeak, he pushed it open. Inside, the air was hot and stale, the floor dust-covered. My eyes grew accustomed to the light and I saw there were no furnishings within the building, no bags of stored goods or trace of habitation.

'What is this place?' I asked, looking up at a roof and the shafts of bright light that penetrated the darkness in which we stood.

'This is the gateway leading beyond the walls. As I said, it is concealed.' He glanced around, the memory of an errant youth in his eye. 'I haven't used it in years.'

Zenobia surveyed the room, her face hardening. She knew as well as I what this could mean. We had experienced much these past years. We had both watched Julius go south; both experienced the worry for a father. Together we had travelled across the empire, to Rome. We had seen the centre of the world and overcome every obstacle to bring home a force large enough to defeat the enemy. We had given the past years in the service of our king and our emperor; Zenobia giving both mind and body, and secured a large force in order to defeat the Persians. And we could lose it all because of the citizens of Antioch.

'There are no guards here?' Zenobia said.

'They are on the outside of the wall,' Bamdad replied.

Zenobia nodded to Bamdad and we followed him through the dim and abandoned rooms, rat skeletons crunching beneath our feet, the stench of any decay long gone. A moment later, a circle of light shone ahead. Bamdad stretched out his arm, halting us. He whistled, paused.

Silence.

'What is wrong?' I asked.

'It is our warning,' he said. 'When we approached, we whistle to alert the guard we are coming. They should signal back to say everything is clear.'

'And yet they have not,' Zenobia said.

'No,' he replied, confusion and concern creeping into his rough voice.

He drew his sword. I did the same, the blade hissing a sweet breath, ready for what may come and the blood it craved. I glanced down at it. There was no trace of the lives it had taken, no nick upon the fine blade, nor blood crusted to the hilt.

A cold hand touched my own.

'Take care, Zabdas,' Zenobia said, her other hand touching her swollen belly. Gods, I thought, what Odenathus would say if he saw us there, what punishment he might inflict knowing I had taken Zenobia to the brink of the city, to a secret gate leading beyond the wall. I wondered for a heartbeat which I feared more, Odenathus or the Persians.

Bamdad and I moved toward the illuminated doorway,

blinking in the harsh light. There was no sound or movement, no sign of disturbance, no smell of sweat-coated Persian. Once outside, the ground sloped down and away, the craggy hillside moving freely beneath my feet and I lost my footing and was surprised and annoyed that it was Zenobia who grabbed my arm. I dared not make a sound, hidden by bushes and trees and thick green leaves, a wall of nature to cover the hidden passage.

A movement. A flick of something beyond the shrubs, light and dark.

I moved forward, knowing as I did so we were not alone, parting the undergrowth with my hand, careful to keep my sword from site for fear of catching sunlight.

'Where are the guards?' Zenobia whispered.

As the words left her lips I found them.

'Here.'

Zenobia's breath felt heavy and hot on my neck as she peered over my shoulder, Bamdad beside me, to see the guards: two men, throats slit, half-hidden in the undergrowth.

'I must inform Odenathus. Zabdas, Bamdad, hold the passageway. Ensure no one comes through.' The commands came easily from her lips. Bamdad frowned, but he accepted her authority with a nod as Zenobia hurried back through the entrance. How we would hold the passageway if the Persian force came, only the gods knew.

We stood in silence. The smell of shit hung feculent and fresh. The sun crept lower and the hillside took an orange glow. I saw the moon, a quiet sliver of the coming night creeping into the day as the enemy slunk their way into Antioch, Bamdad and I the only men standing between the Persians and the gateway into the city. I wondered if a citizen had betrayed their own people, the people of Syria and the army of Rome to the enemy, or whether the Persians had found the entrance by chance. I thought of Palmyra and her beauty and could not resist reflecting on how angry I would be if I were stood in Palmyra now, defending her walls as she bowed beneath the same threat;

betrayed in the same way. Rage boiled. We were one people: Romans, Palmyrenes, men of Antioch. We had been betrayed. Bitterness stung as I looked into Bamdad's face and saw his worry for what would come. I went to speak, but Bamdad let out a long, low hiss as he listened for sound.

'Someone approaches,' he murmured.

Footsteps crunched. I could see nothing from my position, yet I dared not move. Footsteps again, then hushed voices. More than a couple of men. I shifted to maintain the blood flow in my legs. I needed to be ready.

'They are preparing for a night attack?' I mouthed.

Bamdad shook his head and mouthed back: 'Poison more wells. Ruin our stores.'

I caught a flicker of light on iron; of men gathering a hundred feet from us. They crept closer, silent but for the crunch of stone beneath feet and the dull chink of weapons.

Then I heard the Persian tongue.

'Gods' mercy,' Bamdad, his voice little more than a breath on the calm air, echoed my thoughts. Two swords stood between this horde and destruction.

Bamdad plucked my arm and we crept back toward the sanctuary of the city.

There had been no exertion, yet I breathed hard, the enemy just feet away.

'They'll wait till dark,' Bamdad said.

'What do we do?' I said. I racked my brains for a way to slow them enough to allow our army to move and build a suitable defence.

Bamdad shifted his sword from one hand to the other, then back again, over and over. I thought he might suggest we stand and fight, hold the gate until our own forces arrived, die in the attempt to keep the enemy out. But he sheathed his blade.

'We must close the gateway,' he said, looking around him.

A short sigh of relief and I sheathed my own sword as we retreated back into the city street.

'Zabdas?'

Zenobia hurried toward me, her unborn heavy in her belly, her movement awkward and breath short and laboured. Perspiration glistened on her brow. Beside her, Odenathus strode with heavy steps. Behind him, four of his personal guard and a unit of soldiers.

I have a curt nod as he approached.

'Gods be damned, my pregnant wife should not have been here,' he said to me. 'We will talk of this later.' He flicked a hand and the soldiers formed a shield wall before the passageway. 'You are the Syrian?' he demanded of Bamdad, then without waiting for reply said: 'Why was I not told of this entrance sooner?'

I could see the bristle, the tone of the king's voice sitting uncomfortably with Bamdad. Finally, he dipped his head and did not look up as he said, 'I do not know, Lord King.'

'Tell me what you know,' Odenathus replied.

'We have seen a force, my Lord,' Bamdad went on, 'gathering beyond the walls. We suspect they're waiting for nightfall to enter the city.'

Zenobia glanced to the passageway and the men with spears and swords waiting. Her cheeks were red, expression determined.

I could sense Odenathus' desire to put his head in his hands and weep for the stupidity of the citizens who had not told him of this entrance. But he did not let the notion overwhelm him. Instead he stood tall and looked the wall up and down.

'This wall,' he said.

'My Lord,' Bamdad acknowledged.

Odenathus grunted. I waited for him to say something more, but no words passed his lips.

Zenobia said, 'The emperor talks of abandoning the city.'

My ears deceived me, I thought, but realised immediately they had not. Disbelief coursed over me, but then in the shadow of the moment I knew it was true.

'But why?' I said.

Odenathus' grave face could meet neither my eyes nor his wife's.

It was Zenobia who spoke.

'Valerian Caesar believes we people of Syria have betrayed him. He has been persuaded that the water supply has been poisoned by the citizens in order to rid the city of him and his men, and that our supply ships are afraid of coming upriver, rather than blocked. He feels that staying within these walls will bring nothing but death to his empire.' Another man may not have noticed it, but I saw the mask begin to slip from her face and glimpsed the loss of composure which lay beneath.

'And how does he intend to leave?' I asked. 'We will be slaughtered.'

'The Persian's main force is on the east side of the river. We can leave by the other gate, force an exit and head for the mountains.'

'You think we should leave?' I could not believe that Zenobia would consider such a course, that she would not be more willing to stand and to fight.

'There is no choice.' Odenathus said. 'If Valerian leaves with his armies, the Palmyrenes and men of Antioch will be left to stand alone. We are not enough to hold the city and our water supply is already poisoned.'

I looked up at our king, seeking some words of solace, words of certainty. But his face was flushed with embarrassment. He had no faith in his own words, nor did he agree with the emperor's decision any more that Zenobia did, any more than I did, and yet still he would not move his stance. He would toe the Roman line no matter what future it would bring. He would remain a friendly king in a client kingdom. He would carry on whoring himself to the emperor of Rome.

I had once hated Odenathus, indeed I hated him still, for his connection with Zenobia, his placing a child in her belly, for sending Julius south to fight to Tanukh, away from me when I had only just begun to know him. I knew that it was Julius, not

Odenathus, who refused me permission to go south, yet in that moment I not only hated Odenathus, but I despised him for his alignment with Rome; for what I saw as a betrayal of his own people.

'What of the citizens? What of my family?' Bamdad spat. He stood before the king of the east, his posture a challenge.

'The people are free to go with us,' Odenathus replied, his voice deliberately clipped, hiding something more than embarrassment.

I watched the king's internal struggle with a sense of grim satisfaction. Bamdad had confronted him as I had long wanted to face him, Odenathus, King of Palmyra, Ruler of the East. Odenathus was giving the people of Antioch two choices; leave the city, your home and your lives, or stay and face the mercy of the Persian invaders.

CHAPTER 4

Zabdas – 258 AD

Screams sounded, but not close. They were on the west side of the city, telling of a renewed attack on our walls.

'Go back to our lodgings,' Odenathus said to Zenobia. 'I must ensure this route into the city is blocked and buy us the time to leave. I will come for you.'

I looked into her eyes, disbelieving as I saw her guilty resolve.

'Odenathus is right,' she said. 'We must think of what is best. We will die in Antioch if we choose to stand alone. The Roman army is under the command of Valerian and the Roman generals, and they would see the city abandoned. If we stay, we fight alone, and there are not enough of us to face the Persians. There is no hope left here.' Her eyes pleaded. 'Come with me.'

She held out her hand, but she must have known what my response would be. I could not hide from the enemy with her as my fellow warriors faced the enemy.

'I will stay,' I replied.

Zenobia's voice was stern. 'Zabdas, come with me now.'

'Zenobia, go back to the house,' Odenathus said. 'Zabdas, go with her. Guards,' he called behind him, and his four personal guards stepped forth.

Damn it, I thought, as we hurried back through the streets, Bamdad with us.

Zenobia squeezed my hand as we walked. I did not know

why. Perhaps reassuring me that it would all play out, that the city would not fall, that we would be saved. But we both knew that was not to be.

'When the time comes, we must all go,' Bamdad said. 'First I must go to my family, to ready ourselves.'

Zenobia nodded. 'Stay safe, Syrian.'

He winked back at her. 'I always do.'

Two days later the Persians made a hole so wide in the outer wall with their catapults that we had no choice but to abandon the city, no matter what Valerian might have chosen to do.

I was on the training ground with Bamdad when we heard the news. Sweating and grunting, I lunged and cut and parried. He was older, yet I was no match for the strength in his arms or the sense of anticipation he had come to learn over the years.

'You'll not kill many Persians with a cut like that, boy,' he said.

'I am growing faster; you are only getting slower, old man.'

He barked a manic laugh. And I caught his leather covered breast with the tip of my sword. It scored a mark, but did not break through.

'So you are,' he said, 'but not stronger.'

He crashed his sword into my shield, his full strength behind the blow, and I buckled beneath the force of it.

A boy's voice screamed and I looked up from behind my shield.

'They are in the city. They are in the city,' the boy said, running onto the training ground, addressing the hundreds of soldiers stood there. 'The emperor has ordered everyone to evacuate on the west side of the city.'

'Fuck the gods. What a day to flee,' Bamdad said, looking skyward.

'I must go to Zenobia. Ensure she leaves safely. 'And Aurelia,' I added as an afterthought.

'Where are they?'

'The east side.' I pulled the leather cover that I had used during training from my sword to reveal the grey metal beneath.

'My family lie to the south,' Bamdad said.

'Then I will see you at the gate, old man,' I replied.

I nodded, safety bidden with unsaid words. I ran fast, suddenly desperate to reach Zenobia and Aurelia. Roman soldiers already moved through the streets, herding men like cattle, heading for the gate through which they would flee. I forced a path through the tide of armoured men as the city screamed and my own panic welled.

My pounding heart shook my entire body as I pushed through soldiers and women and children and livestock. I found the place where we had stood at the walls, watching the Persians beyond our arrow range, now littered with discarded water-skins. The archers had stood down.

A thudding, heavy and deep, sounded as the Persians rammed the gates nearby. It would not be long before they broke through.

I had not reached Zenobia when I found Aurelia, our belongings bundled in her arms, her delicate face drawn with panic.

'Zabdas!' she cried.

'Where is Zenobia?' I shouted above the noise.

'With the king.'

I put my arm about her shoulders and guided her back through the streets.

More men and women ran across our path, arms burdened with possessions, treasures they did not wish to leave behind; everything they could carry. Children were dragged from their homes crying and women wept as soldiers hurried rushed them on, desperate to leave the city.

Some citizens stayed, peering out of windows, hiding from crowds, trusting in their trade to see them living safely beside the Persians. Aurelia leant into me, flinching, cowering from the noise and disruption. Had Bamdad, found his family? Had he left the city and headed for the hills? I looked into the face of each soldier we passed, searching for familiarity or recognition. I wanted to ensure all those I called friend were safe.

I spotted a girl with long hair, caught the scent of floral, sweet-scented oils and thought it Zenobia. When she turned I saw tears and swollen cheeks, but not my cousin, my half-sister, the queen.

I feared the iron-cased enemy more with every corner we turned. I squeezed Aurelia's shoulders, drawing her nearer to me, pressing her against me, as if it would see her safe. My senses heightened, hoping vigilance would keep me alive.

A young boy pulled at his mother as she struggled with sacks so large she could never carry them out of the city. The boy looked up as we approached. He pulled his mother harder at the sight of me. She brushed him off and tears trickled down his nose, and she seemed not to notice the boy tremble as Aurelia halted.

'You must leave the city now,' she said to the woman as she tried to prise the much beloved sack of belongings from the woman's fingers.

The woman grunted in response, pushing Aurelia aside. She struggled on, and the boy's wails heightened, and Aurelia stooped to his height and said, 'Come with us.'

He shook his head wildly, clinging to his mother.

'Leave him, Aurelia. We have no time for this.'

Despair and hopelessness filled her wide eyes, driven by a heart large enough even for these people; those unwilling to save themselves. I could not watch it, the pain in her face, the distress of leaving a small boy to Persian mercy. I sheathed my sword.

With rough hands I lifted the woman from where she stooped and shook her.

'You must leave now. The enemy is already inside the city. If you do not leave, you will not only lose your possessions, but your son, your virtue and your freedom.'

Her eyes locked on mine.

Wordlessly, her lips a tight line, she opened the precious sack and rummaged inside, pulled out jewels and bottles of swirling liquid and stowed them upon her person. With a last look of disdain, she grabbed her son's arm and heaved him off, disappearing into the crowd.

I put my arm around Aurelia and moved on, pushing through the streets, past carts and horses, trekking endlessly to reach the gate on the west wall. People swarmed around us, all pressing to reach and squeeze through the small gateway and on to the hill-ridden land beyond. I scanned the crowds ceaselessly for Bamdad and his family, hoping that he had found them. Hoping he sought safety. We were shoved, pushed, squashed in the mess of humanity. Aurelia clung to me. I looked over my shoulder, fearing the Persians would come at us whilst we were trapped inside the city. And yet I knew they would not. The citizens would turn a good profit at a slave market, yet the Persian army was not like ours. Theirs was made up of a mixture of men—and some women—and they were disorderly and ill-trained and greedy. They were here for plunder, nothing more. By now they would be raiding the homes and buildings all across the east side until there was nothing left.

We gathered north of the city, lost souls in a barren land, not quite knowing what to do or where to turn next. Our departure had not been planned, as we had wanted it to be. We had not left by choice. We fled the city at a time dictated by the hole punched in Antioch's walls. I was angry. I wanted to know how we could gain victory and take back what was ours, but how could anything be victorious now? We had lost Nisibis, Carrhae, Edessa and many more, and now we had lost Antioch. How much could we lose before there was nothing worth fighting for? The city should have proved a sanctuary, yet it had proved another blow, an ebb in army morale, a failure for the emperor.

A handful of Persians screamed and laughed and taunted us as we fled the city, spitting and cursing and throwing stones and bread and pots after us. But most were content to squabble over the riches we left behind. Everything seemed a blur as I pushed

Aurelia onwards, hoping that Zenobia was safe, knowing it was not just my duty as the royal guard that spurred thought of her.

Darkness fell, a cold blanket to cover the day. We stopped at the roadside, breathless, hungry, a bedraggled band of men, woman, children, soldiers, all moving to where more Roman legions had been stationed in the north, a faint hope that they would provide protection forcing our legs to carry us onwards.

I looked back to Antioch. A fire, fierce and bright against the blackness. Screams carried on the wind. How easily we had been defeated. How quickly. Beside me, Aurelia shivered.

'People still flee,' she said.

I squinted, looking more carefully into the darkness, at the movement in front of the flames. I saw them, moving, bags on backs and children on shoulders; the last people to leave.

'They are lucky the Persians do not have them in shackles.'

She rested a head on my shoulder. 'It was a beautiful city.'

'No longer,' I replied.

We caught up with Zenobia and Odenathus on the road the following day.

'Valerian rides ahead,' Odenathus told us. 'He has despatched riders with the aim of reuniting the scattered factions of the army.'

'You have seen him?' I asked.

'After leaving the city. He is panicked, and he has received information that the Goths press his troops hard in Anatolia.'

'He is weak,' Zenobia said. 'And he will desert us given the chance. We must push the Persians back.'

We walked, Zenobia too, and I worried for her. Her stomach bulged with two thirds of her pregnancy gone, her tired and pale face bearing an expression that betrayed her discomfort. It was to be expected and yet I wished she would ride or sit in a cart instead of continuing on foot.

'We cannot maintain control of a single city,' I retorted. 'What hope is there of pushing them back?'

'It does not matter what we hope for, only that we must,' she said. Her pace slowed a little, and Odenathus took her elbow.

'Ride,' he said.

She shook her head. 'I cannot. It is better to walk.'

A day and a night passed and more soldiers came into sight. I breathed relief, for our company was small for such times. As we neared the groups of soldiers, we saw Romans and Syrians and Valerian himself. We moved on, pushing hard, eager to reach the safety of city walls, until finally we came to rest far north of Palmyra, in Edessa.

'Valerian has called for council,' Odenathus said. 'I must go.'

We were in the house of the city commander, eating his bread and drinking his wine. I looked out of the window, observing people milling in the dark street below. I heard Odenathus' footsteps leaving and turned from the window. I had thought Zenobia would go with him, but she said nothing. A slight sheen covered her forehead, her skin pale and her eyes tired. She moved, adjusting herself, then moved again, her discomfort obvious.

'What is it?' I asked.

'He moves,' she said.

'The baby?'

'He is strong.'

She put a hand on her stomach and sighed. She walked across to the bed. With each step pain flashed across her face. She was so incredibly young, I thought, and her husband so very old. I saw no happiness in her face, only weariness, and I could not help but blame Odenathus. She should have been happy, like her father and Meskenit or me and Aurelia, but I convinced myself she was not. The toil of her reign beside Odenathus, of her responsibility as the wife of a king, and the ambitions she harboured were heavy.

Zenobia lay down and closed her eyes.

'Let her rest,' Aurelia said.

As we walked back to our own room, Aurelia said, 'She should not have walked so far. Not so late in her pregnancy.'

'The king will have an heir soon.' I could not hide the bitterness from my voice.

'The king already has an heir,' Aurelia snapped, the hurt in her voice told me she thought my tone aimed at her.

'I did not mean … my apologies.'

I pulled her to me and drew in the scent of her hair.

'We will have children of our own one day,' she said, 'and the palace in Palmyra will ring with their laughter.'

'But Herodes could be killed in battle. A king always needs more than one son.' I was unable to shift my thoughts. The heirs of Odenathus played in my mind.

We reached our room and I pulled on a cloak and went out into the night.

Unease had built in me since leaving Antioch; something I could not explain. Soldiers kept watch over the city perimeter, but inside the walls all was quiet. The Persians had sacked the city a few months earlier. I could see their plundering in the broken architecture of the commander's house and felt sorrow for the craftsmen who had spent years creating such beauty. I thought of Odenathus as he had stood at the edge of our camp each night on the road to Edessa as I stood guard and tried to make a certain sense of what had happened, where we had found ourselves. I had seen the king awake many times when others lay curled in their beds. Part of me sympathised, but another part of me, the part which held love for Julius, told me he was a coward for not standing apart from Rome.

I walked through the courtyard and breathed the scent of the plants, reminding myself of the garden Julius so dearly loved, picturing Meskenit tending the flowers, savouring the moonlit delight, the only sound the soft pad of my feet on stone blocks. Jasmine and other sweet smells filled my senses, and the whole place appeared to glitter, though no statues or busts remained. Nothing of value had been left within the walls and I became suddenly aware of the emptiness around me.

My heart beat slowly yet more strongly, as if full of the sadness we had all felt as Antioch fell. I could not separate myself from this sadness, only let the thud in my chest accept it, embrace is, drive it round my body until it became a part of me, until I realised what it meant to know loss.

Screams. Loud and long and groaning.

The sounds came from the house.

I ran back, through the heavy wooden door, slamming it into a slave, running through the house, taking the steps two, three at a time, crashing into Aurelia at the top.

The horror and fright on her face checked me. I pushed past her and into Zenobia's room.

Sweat poured from her brow. She screamed again, teeth clenched tight together. Hand clutching a hard stomach, blood … blood covering the sheets, her gown, a great pool of crimson red.

I had crossed the room without realising it and grabbed her hand from her stomach. She near broke my fingers, her grip was so tight.

'Gods,' she screamed. 'Selene. Save my boy.'

She tipped her head backwards, grimacing.

A slave rushed in, bowl of water in hand.

'Where is the physician, the midwife?'

'They have been sent for,' the slave-girl said, her head low, and I felt guilt suddenly for my tone.

More slaves entered, carrying sheets and water.

'He is coming,' Zenobia said.

At first I thought it a question, then I realised she meant the baby.

'He is coming,' she said again.

She looked at me, eyes locking on mine, and I saw real fear in them for the first time.

Zenobia slept. I watched.

I could not see her face from where I sat, only dark hair falling and the silhouette of her figure beneath silken sheets. I felt a chill, and shivered before walking across to her. I perched on the edge of the bed, brushed her hair away from her cheek and whispered her name.

She was pale in the wan light, but she did not wake. I nudged her shoulder. Nothing. It felt as though my heart beat in my throat. The events of that night meant I could not sleep, could not still myself or rest. I was awake, but I was not. In control, yet racing inside myself, trying to keep balance and order.

I placed both hands on the bed and leaned close to listen for breath. I heard a low, shallow sound, and my heartbeat settled. Her eyelids flickered in sleep. She had been given a draught by the physician to aid her slumber, but I was sure it did nothing for the dreams she must have.

I went to stand, to call a slave to fetch the physician back, to have him sit in her room as I did, to watch over her.

'For the love of the gods, what has happened?' Odenathus stood in the doorway of the room, voice echoing in anger and confusion.

I could not speak. My tongue could form no words.

Odenathus looked at Zenobia.

We had stripped the sheets and sent them for burning, dragged in a new mattress from another room and covered it in clean linen. Yet now it was red once more, pooling dark around her, unstopping, uncontrollable, like water slipping between fingers. I feared for her, for her life. But more than that, I was terrified of a future without her, not just for myself, but for everyone, for the whole of Syria. She had become a rock to the people of this country, a steady mind and will of iron that kept us going, that inspired hope where there was none, for her defiance would not let it fade.

Odenathus crossed to her side and peered down at her still form.

I felt as though I should leave them, but I did not want to go, nor could I summon the will to move from her side, no matter the courtesies I owed my king. I stayed there beside them, watching Zenobia beneath her husband's gaze. I wanted to shout, to scream that this was *his* fault. I blamed him for everything that I hated, and now Zenobia lay on a bed, closer to death than I could bear.

Laughter sounded from the courtyard below, jarring and strange. Then I heard Zenobia's laugh in my memory. It seemed more distant now than ever.

Odenathus leaned over her. 'My dear Zenobia.'

My. She was not his, she belonged to no one. Tears stung my eyes as I thought of how little he deserved her. How much I loved her. How quickly I had come at her cries.

'My Lord,' the physician appeared behind us. 'She has lost much blood and is very weak. Death could yet claim her.'

Odenathus appeared unable to utter any sound.

'What has caused this ailment?' he finally managed to ask, voice strained and distorted.

'Her condition in the morning will tell us more.'

'What happened?' Odenathus asked again.

The physician shook, his beard quivering.

'The child did not survive, my King. Indeed, it very near killed her.'

As he spoke, the scrap of flesh, so small, so perfectly formed, born into the world without ever taking breath, burned in my mind. I scrunched my eyes, trying to rid myself of the image, but it refused to shift or to fade.

Odenathus gave Zenobia an unreadable glance and then he was gone.

The physician scrutinized her further.

'She still bleeds,' I said. 'Can you not stop it?'
'I have packed to stem the flow. I only hope it is enough.'
'She cannot die. Syria needs her. The people need her.'
'You must get some rest. I am here to watch over her.'

I nodded, without intention of leaving Zenobia's side until she woke. I felt limp with failure, trying to determine what had been the cause: the walk from Antioch to Edessa; the losses our army had suffered; my own feelings toward her marriage to Odenathus and the child she had subsequently carried …

The physician went to prepare further draughts that he hoped would aid her recovery. I sat down beside her on the bed. Even then, so drained of life, she was beautiful. Tears streamed down my face as I felt my world disintegrate. It was as though all hope had abandoned glorious Syria; the light and heat and heart of the desert extinguished.

CHAPTER 5

Samira – 290 AD (Present day)

My arms ache and my grip is loose and I fear I might drop our provisions as we struggle back to the boat. I see Bamdad on board and he smiles at me. I smile back. I cannot help myself, he is my grandfather's closest friend; my friend, a man who cares for us yet could not be more carefree. He is a man of the world, a man who enjoys life, who worries little for tomorrow or the day after, or the day after that. He lives now and for this moment alone. Yet I know there is more to him than that, I know now that he once had a family, but I know not where they are. Did he find them, I wonder, as I struggle with sacks of bread? Did they escape Antioch before it fell?

Bamdad's smile fades and I realise my own has gone. He frowns at me, and I could laugh at that as I laugh at many things with Bamdad. He disappears from the side of the ship and in a moment reappears, heading down the gangplank, hurrying to help, taking from me the largest sack of bread.

'Gratitude,' I say.

'Have no worry, *Rubetta*, I am always here to help.'

'Are we ready to leave?' grandfather asks.

'As soon as we're all on board,' Bamdad replies.

We board the boat and I find myself face to face with Rostram, the captain, a man I know to be a slave-trader and a pirate; an old friend to my grandfather. He is a little shorter than Bamdad, his hair soft and brown. His eyes hold mine a moment and then he stands aside and with a brief flick of his hand bids me pass.

I am unsure of him, and I do not agree with his trade. Of the enslaving. Grandfather and I had been taken as we journeyed north on the river, taken because the captain of that ship knew my grandfather, knew of the ransom upon his head for killing Jadhima, King of the Tanukh. And the slaves who had been on that ship when Rostram freed us had in turn been freed, and his words ring in my ears, *they have you to thank for that*. He would not have given them their freedom. He would have kept them in chains, sold them on, made a profit from their lives. And yet because of me he let them go, and I cannot fathom why that would be.

Later, I sit with my grandfather. We play dice, pebbles our coin, as the boat moves steadily downriver. I am not winning, despite my grandfather trying to let me, but this is no game of skill or intention, simply one of chance and luck.

'I have read your recent pages,' I say, meaning the papyrus he had scrawled upon this afternoon.

'And what did you make of it?' he asks.

'Zenobia's child did not survive?'

'No.'

Grandfather's face is shadowed by the dying sun and by the memory of the day he sat beside Zenobia, watching her close to death. I have known of many women in Tripolis die in childbirth, and the fear of it haunts us all, but I am not with a man, and I have no child inside me, so for me that fear can wait for another day or month or year.

'She had professed that her son would be the ruler of Syria and Egypt, but it would not be that child.'

'Then it would be another?'

'Perhaps.'

I roll my eyes as him as I roll the dice. Everything must be

Samira - 290 AD (Present day)

told in order, nothing out of place, no hint or whisper of what might have happened on another day, in another year.

'Was she really descended from Cleopatra the Great?'

'Ah; her royal lineage. The claim that she was descended from Dido, Queen of Carthage, Sampsiceramus, King of Emesa, and Cleopatra VII, the last Pharaoh of Egypt. She could have been. I certainly believe so. She was convinced of it, without any doubt.'

What it would be like, I think, to have the blood of the greatest figures of history running through you, the royalty of ancient Egypt, the blood of kings and of queens. It is no wonder that she married a king, become queen herself, found a power that her ancestors had known.

My grandfather smiles as he studies me.

'Roll the dice,' I say with a playful frown.

'All right.' He shakes the cup and spills the dice on the table.

'Did Valerian ever make a stand against Shapur?' I ask. 'Or did he just keep backing away?'

'There was very little direct conflict at that point. The Persians were content to raid where they could without having to engage our full army, and Valerian was too inexperienced and too scared to put a stop to it. Our generals and Odenathus tried to advise him that it was essential we push the Persians back, but Valerian waited, forcing us to retreat all the while. There were small skirmishes, but nothing large scale.'

I am nodding, slow and careful, thinking what it would mean, wondering if they would ever defeat their enemies, ever rid the lands of Persians and find peace.

'Did the Persians win?'

He shakes his head and I know he is considering his answer, that it is not straightforward and that he does not wish to tell too much, out of order and out of time.

'It is complicated to explain. Palmyra and indeed Syria faced many threats from the Persians during the years following Valerian's arrival in the east. We had our defeats, and we had our victories. Many from the Persians, some from the Tanukh, a few from other tribes and warlords staking claim, and of course there were those from the Romans themselves. We were not beloved of Rome,' he says bitterly. 'We were an outpost. Nothing more.'

The boat moves north as grandfather continues the tale of Zenobia; his last duty to a land gone forever, now a land that I know, a land in which I have grown older. A land I have never known to be any different, and yet it must have been, for he remembers, he holds images of another Syria, of great palaces of marble and of kings and queens ruling a desert oasis surrounded by blood and sand.

A picture I can only conjure in my imagination.

CHAPTER 6

Zabdas – 258 AD

Two days passed. More people came, visiting the girl whose face grew paler with the rising and setting of each sun. Her ladies muttered in fear. Aurelia flitted in and out, casting glances at me, worried or angry I did not know. I was never sure, not now, not ever I conceded.

Aurelia helped the physician tend Zenobia. I noted her caring touch, hands that cleaned and cared and nurtured the life left within. But it did not stop my worry and with each day I grew more conscious of Zenobia's deterioration.

Aurelia brought food with every visit, but I could eat nothing, and began to feel my strength drain and muscles waste as I languished day after day in despair. It was not until that moment, sat beside her bed, the world moving on without her participation, that I realised how much she truly meant. I always thought of her as being a queen of the people, and she was, but their world would continue without her presence, Odenathus at the helm, the Empire ever there, lingering to the west. But my world could not move without her. I was trying and failing to be useful, to bring her back from the brink upon which she lay balanced, too far from us, from me, from any helping hand. I did not love her like I loved Aurelia, I did not desire her in the same way and nor did I know the same ease and conversation and warmth with Zenobia, but she belonged in my life more than any beloved sister. She was my family, and I felt as though I failed Julius – myself – with every moment she lay close to death.

Odenathus failed to return. Zabbai told me he was caught in matters of war, but I could scarce believe him so short of time that he could not sit beside his wife.

'You are still here,' Aurelia said as she placed a bowl of water on the table beside Zenobia's sleeping form. She wrung out a cloth and began to bathe her arms.

'There is little for me to do other than be here,' I said.

'I know. I spoke with Zabbai. He says that you have been relieved of any other duties to be here to watch over Zenobia. But please listen, you need to return to your own bed and sleep. You are tired and worn and I am worried for you. I realise you are close, and you feel as though you have failed her, but this has to stop. Come back, Zabdas. Come back to me.'

Her pale face, as tired perhaps as my own, looked down at me and guilt bit. I had immersed myself in my own pain, my own self-pity. Is this what Zenobia would have wanted? I thought not.

'I worry about you, Zabdas,' she continued. 'Both you and the king need to sleep, to rest, or I fear you will be of no use to anyone.'

'Odenathus? He has not even been here,' I spat. 'How can he lose sleep?'

Aurelia studied me, her blue eyes soft and understanding.

'I hear that he has worries for both Zenobia and the army. I have seen his tired eyes and the worry upon his face. He cannot bear what has happened, but he can do nothing, just as you can do nothing. And he is powerless over what is happening to his army. He loves Zenobia, no matter how much you may persuade yourself he does not. His responsibilities are great, and he has much to contend with. Do you not think he would rather sit here, beside his wife?'

'His responsibility is to his wife. It is she who needs him.

Let the emperor defeat the enemy as he ought to.' I held my head in my hands and took a long breath. 'Not once has he been to see her.'

'Perhaps not, but he knows of her condition each hour.'

I sensed my inner fight, unsure whether I believed, unwilling to accept her words.

'I am sorry,' I said at last, and fell silent, not caring to exchange more bitter words with my lover. I buried my head in my arms, hoping she would leave, that I might control once more my emotion.

When I thought her gone, I lifted my head and looked over at Zenobia, the light dim and mistrusting. I moved to Zenobia's bedside and stared at her a while. I felt embarrassment and shame at my actions. I worried not just for Zenobia, but for myself. I felt frightened and alone as the world around me changed, shifting into a new order.

I took her hand and gripped, hoping to gain comfort, but her skin was cold.

The following day, Zenobia's condition became public.

The whole city appeared to know, and I could not help but eye the servants and slaves of the commander's house with contempt. Someone had let slip the cause of her absence, told of the fate of her child, delighted in gossiping to the mob.

Odenathus must have spoken of it, told his generals and they their wives. But I was irrational with grief and foolish in my control, unable to think clearly or to see the world turning around me, moving forward, pressing on as Zenobia and I were shut away. And in my confusion my sense of loss heightened as I began to believe she would never wake. Days passed by in a blur and I knew nothing of the world beyond the walls of Zenobia's room.

A week later and I sat beside the small window, looking out into the garden, absorbed in the silence and the private glimpse of tranquillity, unburdened by soldiers, unspoiled by the enemy. The Persians were believed to be on the move again, having stripped Antioch bare, but we had yet to see their army on the horizon.

'They are fat on Antioch gold,' Zabbai said. 'They are in no hurry.'

'But they will come.' Somehow, I did not care whether or not they came. I could not muster the energy to feel or to think.

'They will,' he conceded. 'Here, I have this for you.' He handed me a roll of papyrus. 'It arrived with some other correspondence for Odenathus.'

I peered down at my name, scrawled finely upon the curved papyrus, and all the worry and anxiety I had known lifted for a heartbeat.

'It is from Julius,' I murmured.

Zabbai said nothing, but looked down at Zenobia's still form.

'You should be training with the other men,' he said.

Forgetting the letter I replied, 'Does Odenathus command me to?'

I could sense by the way he spoke, the unease with which he parted the words, that Aurelia had prompted this conversation.

He shook his head. 'Odenathus would not command that, no, but you have energy born of grief. You would do well to release it. It is advice, Zabdas, nothing more. I do not tell you, only encourage you.'

I wiped my face with my hands, waking a little from my solitude. Zenobia moved, fingers twitching, and my heart thumped quickly in the hope that she had come back to us, but she did not move again.

'Aurelia tells me that soldiers have been dying,' I said.

'Some.'

We both looked at our queen, both, I think, willing the movement to recur, our breath almost held, but not quite.

'Hundreds,' I corrected him absently.

'Perhaps.'

I looked across at him. The teller of truths, yet of late he struggled to tell the whole truth, to avoid awkwardness and simply say what he knew. He wore armour, his chest shining bronze and his face gleaming from the training yard or arguing with the other commanders, I knew not which. But he had changed. There was a respect and a sorrow in him that were known only in this room.

'She is improving?' he asked.

I ignored his question.

Zenobia wore a light shift, clinging to her skin with feverish sweat as her body ran hot and cold. The physician suspected some of her pregnancy might still linger within, prolonging her condition, stalling her recovery. The midwife had come, not long after the physician had packed to stem the flow of blood. She had removed all the wadding and muttered of her uterus and contraction. After a while she refreshed the wadding and told us to pray to the gods. And Aurelia kept telling us that Zenobia just needed a little time, a short rest, and she would be herself once more.

'I hear our men die of plague,' I said, 'and our gods have left us and they have left Zenobia. That we are forsaken.'

My stomach churned with hunger and my head felt light as I stood up.

'A few are dead,' Zabbai replied.

'When we next meet the Persians, our army will not be large enough to defeat them, will it?'

'If the sickness continues, then no, probably not.'

'Why can you not tell the truth?' My voice was bitter.

'You want the truth, Zabdas, open your damned eyes and cease revelling in self-pity. We have spent the last week quarantining the ill in attempt to stop the spread of infection, but plague has taken hold. Who knows how many will die before the Persians come? Half our army? Two thirds? We will no doubt be outnumbered by more than you know, and we will perish. We will die on these sands as Zenobia is dying in this bed. If she was not perishing of childbirth, then she would be suffering like the rest. Our morale is at its lowest. Roman soldiers have been caught deserting. The emperor and Odenathus argue constantly over what is best, and I, quite frankly, am glad of the respite I find when I walk the gardens of this house, despite knowing that as soon as I step into this room I will see a boy pining after his queen and that there is no hope.' He stood before me with clenched fists, spittle on his chin. 'Is that what you wanted to hear?'

I stared at him, at the anger in his face, at his lack of control.

'I cannot think,' I said, and I felt much smaller than I had felt for a long time. It was as if I faced the slave master Firouz once more.

Zabbai placed a hand on my shoulder, shook his head and sighed.

'You feel great loss, Zabdas, because you have known little in this life. You should have something to eat, boy. You are beginning to look paler than your queen.' He gave a short chuckle, intentional, as if trying to lighten the mood.

He turned to leave and Zenobia stirred once more.

Zenobia woke to a land filled with greater fear than I had ever known. Her pale complexion and clammy skin betrayed fever. Her eyes struggled to open, but I saw the glistening blackness beneath her lashes and her hands reached out. I took them, and sat beside her on the bed. I felt tears come, wiped them angrily aside and tried to fix an expression of cheerfulness on my face, to smile and warmly welcome her back from her slumber.

Her eyes opened more fully.

'Zenobia? Can you hear me?' Zabbai said.

She blinked and looked between the two of us, moving her fingers, arms and feet.

'I hear you,' she said, her voice cracking and fragile.

She tried to sit up.

'Lie down,' I said, and put a hand on her shoulder.

'I am well enough. A little tired,' she said. 'That is all.'

'We thought you would die.' It was my voice which cracked as I spoke.

'I have lost the child?' she said, matter of fact, no preamble or pause, no tears or emotion.

I nodded.

She put a hand to her soft belly. 'Was it a boy or a girl?'

I could not speak, my throat tight and my mouth unmoving.

Zabbai said, 'A boy. A little too young for this world. And far too young for the next.'

She nodded, accepting his words and the will of the gods.

'I will have another, strong and true. The gods tell me so.'

Her faith in the gods was far greater than mine, far more certain than most. She turned her head toward the window,

'I dreamt of you, Zabdas, many times. I dreamed of Aurelia too. The skies were green-blue and filled with storm clouds. But we were there, alone on the desert plain. I cannot recall the direction we looked, only our being there. And the knowledge came that there would be a new ruler of Syria.'

'Who?' I asked.

'They were faceless.' Her brow creased with the memory. 'And plague took our people, but they were saved by this person, this strong ruler. Where is Odenathus?'

'He is with the men, Zenobia,' Zabbai said. 'It is true. A plague has descended upon the armies of Rome and Syria. Our numbers are much smaller than before. Your husband speaks with the emperor to rectify our situation. We had hoped to strike the Persians as they left Antioch, but hear reports that have left already and we are weakening by the hour.'

'I must see my husband.'

Aurelia rushed into the room, her sandals slapping heavily on the floor, basket of linen in her arms.

'Fetch the physician,' Zabbai said to her.

'Of course.'

'Send someone for Odenathus,' Zenobia said.

'Odenathus has not been here since you lost the child.' I surprised myself at how much satisfaction the words gave me.

Zenobia closed her eyes. 'It matters not, send for him.'

With Zenobia awake, eating and sipping water, I was persuaded to my own bed to rest a while. I had forgotten the letter Zabdas had given me from Julius, Zenobia's own father and husband to my birth mother, Meskenit, but I picked it up before leaving Zenobia's room, the prospect of reading it the reason I had not been so reluctant for time alone.

I felt warm as I touched the same papyrus he had touched, the familiarity and comfort it brought, that the man who had saved me from slavery had written to me once more. It had been only a few months since I had seen him last, the year now drawing to a close, and yet I missed him greatly. I unrolled the message and read the words written in his beautiful hand:

Zabdas,

I hope this letter finds you well. I confess after my brief return home (to Antioch, alas, not Palmyra or my own villa) I have longed to return and never again to leave.

When Odenathus first asked me to travel south to fight the Tanukh, I had expected to return long before now, to fulfil my promise not to leave you in Palmyra. I have been in the south a long time: too long. I am eager to spend time with you, to show you the family life I have before now shared with my daughters. To see you and Meskenit united, and for her to warm to you. I am sorry, that I could not stay longer after giving you the news that she is your mother and not your aunt. It was, I believe, quite cruel of me, and yet unavoidable. Alas, I can do nothing about that now.

I have written to Odenathus with a detailed account of the Tanukh's movement on the Euphrates. They grow stronger, but we are holding them. Their new leader, Jadhima, has taken the title of king; a little ironic considering his tribe is a faction of the Persian Empire. I wonder if Shapur knows of his rival. Both attempt to plunder our wealth, after all.

I have worried about you much, Zabdas. I hope that you are well, that you continue to learn and to grow and that your proximity to Zenobia will keep you safe.

I hear that sweet Hebony has a baby girl and my dearest Zenobia is carrying Odenathus' child! I sacrifice to the gods daily in the hope that she remains in good health and the child is born safely into our world. I hope to travel again, to Palmyra, once Zenobia's child is born, if only for a few days. I hope we will see one another then. If you would like, I shall ensure Odenathus makes it so.

With great affection,
Julius ~

I lay down on my bed and read it again. Then I reread it over and again until the words were committed to my memory and the note was merely an object, a smell, a reminder of the man. I wondered if Odenathus had written to Julius to tell him of his grandson, or whether he would leave that for Zenobia to do.

I stood up and walked across to the table where papyrus and reed waited.

Zenobia became stronger with every hour. She asked how many had died of plague, how many troops were still fit to fight, what words had passed between Odenathus and the emperor. I had spent so much time at her bedside I could not answer her questions, but Zabbai informed where he could.

When Odenathus failed to come, Zenobia insisted she go to him.

'There is much to be done if we wish to survive the Persian threat.'

'You cannot. You were close to death, and you are still weak.'

'Oh, Zabdas. I have spent an age resting, I am eager to be out of this room. I am a woman, but I am a strong one.' She patronized me, but she must have known the words would scorn me into letting her leave. At my frown she sighed.

'You know I will go anyway, so help me up.'

I did as she said, and before long we were walking through the gardens, Zabbai on one side of her and I on the other. I noticed her scent, her skin and hair without oils reminded me of the sea.

We walked out into the street, the stench of death and disease humid and heavy in the air. I recoiled, clapped a hand to my mouth. An oxen-pulled cart crossed our path and we paused, seeing as it passed corpses draping from the back, scarred and mutilated with disease, flies buzzing.

'A few?' I muttered to Zabbai.

'I told you, the death toll increases every day. They burn the bodies outside the city to stop the spread, but it becomes stronger. They are mostly Roman,' he added, as if to provide consolation.

Anxiety stabbed as I thought of Aurelia and her Roman origin. Of whether they were more susceptible to this plague than our own countrymen.

'Let us move on,' I said.

Zabbai led us to the highest point in the city, to a house with a tall façade and bronze statues. I helped Zenobia up the slope to the house, but she pulled away from me, walking alone. The Roman guards let us pass with a curt nod to Zabbai and quizzical looks at Zenobia. Her paleness and concentration on the simplest of steps betrayed her physical weakness. Inside the house were more bronze statues and sprawling mosaics. I heard voices, and we followed them.

'Whose house is this?' I asked Zabbai.

'It belongs to a merchant, but Valerian has taken residence here. Odenathus was heading to see the emperor when I left him earlier.'

We entered another room in which Valerian sat, Odenathus standing before him. They were deep in conversation, and I noted the generals of Rome and the Stratego of the east were also present.

The group turned as we entered, and I started when I saw Bamdad. Relief surged within me. Gods, he was alive, and yet he was dishevelled, bruised, slumping with tiredness. I longed to know what news he had, but it would have to wait as Odenathus turned to his wife, his face relaxing.

'Zenobia, you have woken.' His voice seemed heavy with disappointment.

She looked back at him, her expression indifferent. She might have been weak in body, but her mind had woken stronger than before.

'I am well,' she replied.

Odenathus appeared to want to say more, but instead he turned back to the emperor and generals. Zenobia sat quietly to one side, I stood beside her. Zabbai joined Odenathus. Valerian had looked on Zenobia's appearance with irritation, but now he resumed his conversation with a jerk of his head, as if brushing away a fly.

'So, the man who betrayed Antioch is dead,' Valerian mused. He looked haggard and exhausted. His task in Syria had been a failure since he arrived. He had managed to yield more land to the enemy than Odenathus had ever done, and still our king would not stand against him, still Odenathus bowed to Rome. Did our enemies now suffer plague as we did, were their numbers also diminishing? Could we stand equal, or had we been forsaken? Had the gods truly left us to the mercy of Valerian's ill decision, or indeed the mercy of Shapur?

'True enough,' Bamdad replied. 'The man who led the Persians into the city to poison the water supply is dead; more so than the men on the carts in your streets.' Grief riddled his face and yet he spoke lightly. I longed to know if his family had escaped the city of Antioch. I prayed to all the gods that he had found and them and sent them to safety, away from Antioch and the Persians, away from this place of disease and death.

'You have told us everything you know?' Odenathus said.

'I have.' Bamdad gave pause.

'What is it?' Valerian asked.

'Some suspect the Persians also sent disease into the city to spread sickness. Perhaps the same disease is now killing your men.'

Valerian paled, his eyes panicked, and his hand twitched to cover his mouth, but he dared not show more fear before King Odenathus and his own generals. He would not wish to appear as weak as we knew him to be.

He said, 'You may leave us.'

A man ran into the room. 'Caesar …' he said, voice breathless.

'What?'

'Caesar …' he began again, 'the enemy are on the move.'

Odenathus ordered his stratego to ready our men for battle. Valerian panicked, sending more scouts to confirm that the enemy did indeed approach.

'I have travelled hard for many days to bring you this news,' the messenger insisted. He was young, a little older than me. He walked stiffly and swayed, as if he would collapse at any moment.

'But are you sure?' Valerian demanded.

'Caesar, you must ready your legions,' Odenathus said. 'If the boy is right, we have little time. A defence must be made if we are to survive.'

Valerian's face changed from one of disbelief to shock.

'Come,' Bamdad said to me, and we left the house amidst chaos.

Once outside, Bamdad embraced me.

'He is a weak man, the Roman.'

'He fails to see what is under his very nose. What happened?' I asked, unable to hide my curiosity any longer. 'What happened in Antioch?'

Bamdad sighed and the weight of the previous days seemed to bear down on him.

'I was caught in the press of people leaving the city. It was mayhem. Everywhere soldiers moved and people were in panic. When the streets cleared, I managed to reach our home, but when I got there my wife and children were already gone. I do not know what has become of them.'

Grief and despair showed on his face, and yet I could also see his strength, the soldier inside him.

'They could have left the city before you.'

'I waited for weeks inside the city, hiding where I could, hoping to find them amongst those taken as slaves. Eventually I thought to look for them elsewhere, among the dispossessed, on the roads, heading for another city, but I have not found them.'

I knew then how lucky I was to have left with Aurelia. For her not to have been taken a slave, and for the time I spent wallowing in Zenobia's ill-health, now that she was gaining strength.

'You have my sympathy, Bamdad. If there is anything I can do, you only need to ask.'

'Kill Persians.'

Aurelia placed a cup on the table before Bamdad. The smell of bread hung heavy in the kitchen and my stomach gave a painful rumble.

Bamdad drained his cup and Aurelia refilled it. She touched my arm and gave a sad smile. I felt embarrassed at my proximity to Aurelia, to Zenobia, when he was still in search of his own wife and children.

After a moment I ventured, 'You said that the traitor is dead. Did you mean the person who betrayed Antioch, who told the Persians of the hidden entrance into the city?'

Bamdad stirred from his thoughts.

'They betrayed the entrance to the Persians,' he said, his voice thick and gruff. For a strong man, who had joked and whooped so gleefully in the face of the enemy, it was odd to see him now so distant. He took a deep breath and leaned back in the chair.

Aurelia settled herself opposite, wiped her hands on a cloth.

'The hole in the city wall was swarming with Persians. The gates were eventually opened from within. There were many people still inside the city.' Bamdad shook his head, as if willing himself to go on. 'The enemy poured into Antioch, killing and raping. I heard the screams of my people. So many screams …'

Aurelia shifted beside me. Beneath the table I took her hand in mine.

'I went to my house but my wife and children were not there. And as I left I heard the first cries. Nearby. I heard them again. They pierced the sky, so loud and shrill. I followed the noise to a neighbour's house; an old man and his daughter. He had been a stonemason in his youth, but for some years he had suffered from the wracking cough caused by the dust of his craft. I would hear him in the night, a sound familiar to those in my part of the city. I entered the house with only my sword. More screams came from the darkness. There were men, Persian bastards …' Bamdad looked down at his hands as if expecting to see the blood of the enemy dripping from them.

Aurelia refilled his cup and he snapped from the trance and glanced up at her. He gave me a roguish grin. I smiled back, more because his strange mood disconcerted me than because I shared whatever it was that amused him.

'And the traitor?' I prompted.

His expression turned to one of disgust.

'A week or so after the city fell, the Persians began to drift … some of the citizens were left behind and not taken as slaves: the sick and the dying; those who concealed their presence from the enemy. Even a few traders who had thrown in their lot with the Persians. People came back from the sanctuary of the hills, back to a barren city. Livestock had been taken, food, riches, anything of value. What the enemy couldn't take, they had destroyed.

'One man remained. He was not a Persian, but for all the gods in all the kingdoms, I would name him so. Rumours circulated of a local in league with the enemy; a Syrian who had joined them, and that he had taken residence in the house of the priest king, Haddudan, who is thought to have fled. Those who lost everything sought him out. I was one of those who went to the house, who forced entry to find him with possessions that could only have been bought with blood. He had the only riches left in the city.

'With a sword in my hand and a mind for revenge, I claimed his life. I took his head. Blood still swims before my eyes. I have killed many men, but none with as much hatred as this one. His evil, treacherous blood spurted from his neck and his mouth tried to speak, but nothing came. He could speak no more. He could never again betray Syria.'

'Who betrayed us?' I asked.

'The man …' Bamdad began, but checked himself at the sound of the door opening.

Zenobia came into the room, pale and sickly. Fresh bruising shone on her right cheek and I bristled with rage at the thought that Odenathus had raised his hand to her after her ordeal and her loss. Odenathus was not with her. She clung to the wall, steadying herself, then walked over and took a seat beside me.

'The traitor was Mareades,' she said.

It took a heartbeat for me to recall the city official accused of embezzlement earlier that year. The same man we had suspected innocent but were unable to prove so. The one who had been branded with the slave mark upon his cheek, whom I had persuaded Zenobia to purchase, and who she had subsequently set free.

'But you set him free!' Aurelia said.

My ears deceived me. It could not have been him, not after what we had done, not after I had begged Zenobia for his life. She was mistaken. Confusion took hold and I put a hand on Bamdad's shoulder.

He nodded agreement. 'It was Mareades. Once gone from

the city, he must have headed straight for the Persian army, intent on bringing the city down in revenge.'

'He ought to have been grateful for his life,' I spat. 'How could he do this? To his people? With his own family still inside the city!'

'Revenge was reason enough,' Zenobia said.

'Enough?' I demanded, thumping both my fists on the table. 'You gave him back his life and he betrayed us all. He cared not for us, nor for his fellow citizens, those who would support him if they could. He cared for what? Revenge? On one man? On the priest king who saw him made a slave? Gods' breath, he is a traitor.'

Zenobia sat motionless, her hands placed in her lap.

'He was not free, Zabdas. What he lost tormented him, as it would most men. He lost his home, his family, every possession he owned. Above all, he lost his pride the day he was branded a slave and committed to a life worse than death; to a life of solitude and shame.'

Bamdad looked curiously at this girl with dark, almond eyes and long tumbling hair. His mouth twitched with amusement, to hear such words leave the lips of someone so young.

She continued: 'We could have done no more, but I was foolish to think him shallow enough to accept life at any cost, for him to accept the brand upon his face, and for him live with that. He could have taken his own life, but he did not. I will know better hereafter.'

'Zenobia is right,' Aurelia said ruefully. 'He was never going to accept what had happened. He could never move on.'

In my youth, I was too pig-headed to see what the two women before me understood. Would I have done what he had done? I knew then I would not. But I did not know what I would have done in his position. Find a new life, in the hills? Find contentment as a nomad? Perhaps I was not old enough to know.

CHAPTER 7

Zabdas – 260 AD

THE YEAR CAME TO a close, the next ran its course, and then another began. Months of plague saw our armies weaken further still. Riders returned telling of the proximity of the Persian army as messengers from the west told of the Gothic invasion in northern Anatolia, of Pontus and Cappadocia. Valerian sent his army to Antiocheia to intercept them, but with them they carried the plague and they failed.

Our own soldiers, and those of Rome and every country of the Empire who remained in Edessa, plunged into gruelling training in readiness for the Persian approach, fighting the sickness which very near consumed us. Those who were fit enough trained hard, tried to ease the worries that death itself was now against us. Fear of both a mortal and an immortal enemy seethed, and our numbers shrank to two thirds of what they had been when Valerian Caesar first came to Syria.

Each morning brought news of more deaths, more illness and dying. I had little experience of armies so large, but those men of Rome knew only too well the outcome for a man whose stomach coated the inside of a bucket and could not hold his bowels. They knew those poor souls faced death, and neither strength nor skill in battle could save them.

I longed for a chance to escape the disease infested city, but never did I think of desertion as so many had done. I stayed to face the enemy when they came. It was not long before that opportunity came.

I dressed before the sun rose as I did every day, splashing cool water on my face to revive myself, and I donned boiled leather that had come to fit my shape, stretched with the muscle I had built. I strapped shin guards to my legs, fastening them tight so they would not slip. We wore them every day to train, so that our bodies grew accustomed to the feel and movement within.

A shadow moved behind me as I pulled the straps. Zabbai's tall, hefty frame stood in the doorway, watching me flex to check the tightness of my armour.

'The change of boys into men always astonishes,' he said, judging with seasoned eyes.

'You were once a boy yourself,' I replied, half-laughing. I looked at the muscle on his arms and his broad chest and knew that one day I would look like him, know the ripple of strength beneath sun-marked flesh and the scars of my errors.

'It always amazes me, how quickly the young grow into men.'

'And young men into old,' I chided.

Zabbai smiled.

'Is Zenobia returning to Palmyra?' I asked. After the loss of her child and the revelation of Mareades' betrayal, she and Odenathus had barely spoken. He insisted she return to Palmyra, to the safety of the oasis, to her mother and sister, and, without voicing it, out of his sight and mind.

'She has not left yet. But she will. You are to go with her.'

'I had assumed as much,' I said, but without bitterness, knowing Julius' desire to keep me as far from the frontier as he could. I respected that now. Yet here we were, and here Zenobia was, as near as she possibly could be; as near as she wanted to be.

Part of me hoped she would go soon, because Aurelia would then go too, with her and with me, back to the city I saw as sanctuary, the oasis of my early years as a soldier. Then both would be safe; further from disease and enemies and the Romans.

I fastened the last strap of my armour and then my sword

belt, and turned to Zabbai. His face was creased with age and worry. He had always sided with Odenathus on matters of Rome and the emperor. A loyal friend to the king, as Odenathus was loyal to his overlords. Perhaps, beneath the loyalty he showed, hidden behind his friendship, he agreed with Julius' belief that Syria should be free.

'No need to train today,' he said. 'Odenathus requested I fetch you.' He jerked his head. 'We should go.'

'What does he want?'

'He did not say,' Zabbai replied, 'but asked for us both.'

'A little odd.'

Zabbai did not respond.

'Where is he?'

'With the emperor.'

Guards stood aside once more and we entered the cool, dim interior of the emperor's residence. Both Odenathus and Valerian were in the same room as before. They stood facing one another. Zenobia sat in a chair. Her face, although always long and oval, appeared gaunt with the loss of her child. She propped her head with a fist beneath her right cheekbone, and studied the walls, her eyes hollow and a little lost.

Around them, Praetorian guards watched on.

'You have some objection, Odenathus?' Valerian was saying. 'Am I not gracious? I bestowed upon you the title Illustrious Consul our Lord, did I not? You could want nothing more.'

'You did, Caesar.' Odenathus appeared to struggle between annoyance and respect for his superior. How much further until he broke, the gods may know, but I did not.

'It is not enough to satisfy you?' Valerian pursued.

'I appreciate it well enough. I wished only to express my concern for your proposition,' Odenathus replied.

The king's face was pale, etched with more than worry; an inherent fear of that which he could not control. Although a larger, broader man, Odenathus' frame was slumped, an indication of his willingness to submit.

'You have pushed the boundaries of your leadership much, Odenathus. You were not given the title of king by Rome; you assumed it of your own accord. And yet we said nothing while you styled yourself. Now you dare to question me? If it were not for Rome, not for my allowing your rule, your family would be poorer than the peasants rotting in the gutters of this city.'

Valerian glanced toward us, a flicker in his eyes, words dying on his lips. He grew in height a hand's-breadth, yet Odenathus was not as quick to mask their conversation.

'Sit down,' Valerian instructed.

Zenobia pulled herself upright in her chair. Odenathus took a seat opposite. Valerian took a dozen deep breaths and sat also, his imperial fineries pooling on the couch.

'I have called you here for a specific reason,' Valerian said. 'We have suffered heavy losses both at Antioch and to the plague sweeping through our armies.' He spoke as if it were not his fault; it had been the will of the gods. 'I received reports from my generals last night. We have lost close to a third of the men we brought.'

Odenathus said nothing, looked down at his hands, betraying the fears we all fought, as I wondered what the emperor's admittance finally meant. Zenobia was impassive, unworried, waiting absently for Valerian's next words.

It was Valerian's praetorian prefect, Ballista, who spoke.

'The generals tell us that if we stand against the Persians now, one enemy line against another, we will be outnumbered and likely lose. Roman legions have been sent for, but Rome has many enemies, and much of our forces are engaged elsewhere. I, for one, have no wish to die in the east.'

He smiled. A genial, good-natured smile, as if his words were of little consequence. Our paths had crossed a few times. He was as tall as Odenathus, but wiry thin, black hair so short and fine I could see his scalp. He wore an off-white toga, brightly embroidered bands on long sleeves, and on the shoulder a small scorpion brooch was pinned. Under his toga, the faint hint of a sword showed beneath the linen.

'That is correct,' Valerian agreed. 'There are many enemies, and we are spread too thin at present.'

'What is it you propose?' Zabbai asked.

Valerian's eyes darted to each of us. Purple robes of authority draped his shoulders in a colourful reminder of his position. He clasped his hands in front of him and he cleared his throat.

'There is only one way to proceed. We must seek terms with Shapur.'

'It is the only choice we have,' Ballista concurred.

'I have long thought that we should seek a certain peace, for now,' Odenathus said. 'But what terms is it you wish to seek?'

'That is my concern,' Valerian replied, 'and not the purpose of this meeting.'

'Then what is its purpose?' I asked, perplexed.

'Before peace can be sought, we must arrange a meeting, to discuss our terms, of course, assess if the Persians would be willing. We have attempted to approach Shapur before, and every time my men are sent back without a finger's breadth of skin on them, each one flayed. I doubt Shapur even grants them an audience, let alone reads any correspondence we send, considering how it returns ...' He paused for a moment, a nervousness creeping upon his face. 'I can think of no one better to send than your wife, Odenathus. She proved to me she can speak as well as any man the day she walked into Rome with a handful of men and demanded I tend the east. She holds rank as your wife and favour as a woman, and so we will neither offend Shapur, nor would she come to harm. It is a last resort, but I hope it will suffice. I can allow two soldiers to go with her, so the envoy is not taken as a threat. They may well be more willing to grant you audience. The Persians send Roman messengers back in a worst state than the Syrians, and as Zabbai and Zabdas came to Rome, and my son appears to invest a certain amount of trust in you both, you shall go with her. I presume you would want two men you know loyal to you to accompany her?'

The last was directed at Odenathus. He did not once look at Zenobia as he spoke.

My ears must deceive me, I thought. Our journey to Rome, to request aid for the east, had been a friendly mission. In Rome, we had been in the capital of our own empire, not behind enemy lines.

Zabbai appeared as stunned as I, but Zenobia simply sat in silence, brow creased in thought.

Odenathus said, 'You cannot expect them to go to the Persian camp. They would not return alive. Not with a thousand men to protect them.'

'My guard will see them so far, but then they are alone.'

'I will not allow any wife of mine to go on such a quest,' Odenathus shouted. 'You really think that a queen, a general and a soldier little more than a boy can secure you a meeting to discuss peace? They will be cut down before they even reach their camp. This is madness. Do your own generals, do the senate, know of you plan to negotiate?'

Odenathus' face was red, hot and fiery and full of rage. I had not seen him stand against the emperor before, not bellow or shout or speak with such force. He had always spoken with reason, attempted to persuade, to try and make Valerian understand. Now it was as if a god had let thunder roll through the skies, and I knew then why he was a king.

'It is not wise to question the emperor,' Ballista began.

But Valerian was already on his feet.

'You would defy your emperor?'

He stepped toward the king.

Odenathus looked as if about to retort, then seemed to change his mind and it was as if the life had been drained from him. He had done all that had been requested of him. Why then, send Zenobia? I could understand Valerian's reasons, and yet I could not resist wondering if there was something more, if there was an enjoyment in now sending her and Zabbai and myself to danger, a hark back to our defiance in Rome. Because Zenobia had persuaded Valerian's son, Gallienus, to give us the reinforcements we needed when Valerian would not. And now Valerian stood in the face of defeat, contemplating suing for peace as a last resort.

'Be aware, Odenathus, that you are only king whilst I allow it. You have power through my authority alone.' Valerian took a step closer to him, vehemence in his eyes. 'I am your overlord, do not forget that.'

He spat each word; a last, desperate cling to the power his title gave him. His distrust of Odenathus, the reason he had clawed back the power the king had known, his hostility these long months in the east, now became apparent. He was not only threatened by Odenathus and the power he held amongst the people of Syria, but jealous too. Jealous of Odenathus' fearless skill in battle, the cities he had defended or reclaimed, of his wilful wife, his loyal subjects and, above all, and despite everything, his own loyalty to Rome and the empire.

Odenathus shrank back into his seat. He gave a curt nod.

Zenobia's face betrayed the faint hint of a smile. She rose from the chair, crossed the room to her husband, touched his shoulder in reassurance and turned to the emperor.

'I acknowledge your request. We will leave at first light tomorrow.'

This was the Zenobia I knew, the one who had journeyed to Rome, sought out the co-emperor, Gallienus, and had seventy-thousand men march east to our aid. I knew from the smile which had caressed her lips she always intended to do as Valerian commanded, and in a way that made it her choice, not his, not Odenathus', not any man's.

I glanced at Zabbai, suddenly nervous. We would travel with her. We would face the Persian army. Zabbai responded with a grim look, his features shadowed by the events in this house.

Valerian nodded, clumsy and ill-prepared, Zenobia's

compliance clearly surprising him.

'Very good,' Ballista said. 'I will assist in drafting a message to present to Shapur, and will organise an escort.'

'Gratitude,' Valerian replied, and left the room. Ballista and the Praetorian Guard followed.

Odenathus rose. An argument formed, but he did not speak it. After a wordless moment, he followed Valerian. Only Zabbai, Zenobia and I remained.

'Odenathus is all but beaten.' Zenobia showed little concern as she spoke. Her robes were light and clean. She wore her hair piled high atop her head, held in place with a gold circlet.

'We are all beaten men,' Zabbai retorted. 'How could Valerian seek terms with Shapur now? After all that he has done, after he has caused the failure, indeed the fall, of Syria? It would have been better had he not come to the east, to our homeland. Gods' strength, I am losing my will.'

Zabbai unnerved me. He was always reasonable, level-headed, sure of himself and those he believed in. Yet now he spoke of his own loss of will, and I saw panic in him and it brought in me great fear.

'Will Shapur agree to peace?' I asked.

'Do not be stupid, boy.' Zabbai paused, rage simmering. 'I pray the gods have seen this. If ever we needed their favour, it is now.'

'Shapur will not agree to peace unless enough coin is exchanged,' Zenobia said.

A jug of wine sat atop a marble table. She took it and filled a cup and drank deeply. Despite her sure tone, her hands shook. She offered both Zabbai and me a cup. We took them and resumed our seats.

Zenobia looked down at the wine shimmering in her cup. The trembling of her hands subsided a little, but it did not cease.

'It is nothing,' she said. 'Tomorrow we meet with Shapur, King of the Sassanid Empire. And then we will know where we stand. Whether we can buy the time we need.'

She smiled, genuine and with excitement. I could not help but sense the fear beneath, the shared knowledge of what had happened to every messenger sent before us to the Persian camp. Would we be treated so different? We could, I told myself. Of course we could. I would have Zenobia with me.

'You think we will get to within five hundred paces of him before they kill us?' Zabbai snapped.

'We have to,' she said.

'How much would be enough to secure peace?' I asked.

Zenobia shrugged and drank, deep and long and with a thirst I did not know.

'Everything we have,' Zabbai said. 'Shapur knows we are beaten. We have lost Antioch and we have done nothing more than retreat these past two years. He will ask for nothing less than everything.'

'Then why do you agree to seek terms, Zenobia?'

She took another sip of wine and pressed her lips together. She regarded me.

'Because as the Emperor quite rightly said, we are the best hope of gaining an audience with Shapur and persuading him to meet. Neither Valerian nor Odenathus have sent a female envoy to the Persians. It should make no difference whether I be a woman or a man, but everything depends on whether or not it makes a difference to Shapur.'

'The chances are slim,' Zabbai said. 'And have you not thought, we are to go with you? What is to say you return and we do not? I have no issue in accompanying you for the sake of Syria, if there is a chance you might be able to save our cause, but I am not blind to the outcome.'

'Neither am I, Zabbai. And I owe you a good deal of gratitude for your willingness to put your trust in this,' Zenobia said. 'We are this land's last hope. With us lies the future of Syria, Palmyra, and the whole of the east.'

She curled her legs beneath her on the couch. Her fear appeared to have dissipated and amusement played on her face.

Beneath her elegant confidence, the fear, the excitement, her concerns, worries and hopes, there was something of a plan.

Aurelia did not wish me luck or good fortune. I spent the night holding her, fearful of letting her go, of never returning. Sick at the thought that I would never smell her, sleep beside her, see her pale and wondrous face again. And I thought on Julius, how I might now be in the south with him, and safer for it, than I would be the following day. I feared for Zenobia, whose pride and determination and confidence would see her fall, who could never charm another king the way she had charmed Odenathus and Gallienus in turn. Could not escape the guilt I felt at the thought of Zabbai coming with us, pulled into this as I had been, a man whose body would be flayed on the whim of an emperor.

I was young; I feared death.

If we were lucky, we might die; a sudden, clean death. But we would not simply die. We would be tortured for the amusement of others, and returned home indescribable.

When morning finally came, and Aurelia's tears had dried, and I had come to accept what would become of us, that this night could be the last to feel her warmth, to know her and be with her, a real and tangible part of my life that I had not before now appreciated as I should have, only then did I leave our house and walk toward my fate.

Bamdad had looked upon me with such horror as I told him of what we set out to do. 'You cannot,' he had said. 'It's walking to fucking death.'

I heard those words over and over in his footsteps beside me. I had seen my own fear in his face, stark as the desert, not like Odenathus', nor Zenobia's or Zabbai's fear. In them it had been controlled, but I felt harnessed to it. In Aurelia it had been desperate, almost a fear of fear itself. But in Bamdad I saw shock, and the truth. He did not expect to see me again.

Dawn approached fast. The first stirs of a waking city rustled in the streets. Bakers moving bread to market stalls and slaved washing villa steps.

Aurelia walked with me, Bamdad beside her.

We met at the outer city wall. Zenobia, Zabbai, the camels were already waiting. Three of the Praetorian Guard, fully armoured, red cloaks heavy on their shoulders, were mounted. They nodded acknowledgement as we approached.

I kissed Aurelia. 'I will see you soon. I promise you.' Empty words, but I had no better and nothing more would form. I exhaled, long and low and with sorrow.

Bamdad gave the whole party a look of mistrust. To me he nodded curtly. Then he and Aurelia walked away. I wanted to speak, to form the right words, but they did not come. Instead I turned to Zenobia.

'Where is Odenathus?'

She ignored the question and I knew the tension between them remained.

'Ready?' she asked instead.

Zabbai and I nodded.

A man ran toward us, his tunic off-white, a tube clasped tight in his hand; the message Valerian would have us present to Shapur.

Zenobia gestured he give it to me.

I took the scroll. A seal depicting the emperor's profile looked to the left. I tucked it neatly in the saddle bag of my camel and mounted.

Zenobia clicked her tongue as she glanced back at the city. I suspected she thought to see Odenathus, but he was not there. I wished that Aurelia had stayed, but I knew that it would have made our departure all the harder, and so I followed Zenobia out from the shelter of the walls toward the Persian enemy.

Winter was upon us and the air moist and cold. A chill of the plague we were leaving behind, and the arrival of the early months. We wrapped ourselves in fleece cloaks. The plain was grey and flat, the sky equally lifeless and still. Zenobia rode beside me, her face as cold as the air around us, and beyond her, Zabbai. In front, our small escort provided by Valerian.

'How long will it take to reach their camp?' I asked, breaking our silence.

'Keep moving in this direction and our scouts say we should reach it by nightfall tomorrow, maybe sooner,' Zabbai replied.

We sank into uninhabited land. The closer we came to the enemy, the further we were from home; from retreat. I knew we could not turn back. Even if the desire overwhelmed me, I knew it would not Zenobia, and I knew too that Valerian would be waiting for our return. Take the scroll back, crossed the thought, and tell the emperor that Shapur had no desire to seek terms. He would never know.

We pitched our camp on the plain and our escort bade us farewell. We were alone. Three figures huddled around a meagre campfire. We did not speak. There was nothing to say. Eventually Zenobia got to her feet and stooped into her tent.

Stars grew bright in the darkening sky. Our camels' breathing the only sound above the crackling fire.

'How in the name of Bel did we end we end up here?' I muttered.

'Because the emperor commanded it,' Zabbai said. He sat upright and surveyed the growing blackness. 'We will probably die, Zabdas, but we will die with honour.'

I slept, fitful and with much thought. I could not escape the day ahead. Nor the prospect we faced. For too long I had wanted to be at the frontier, to witness battle, to know what it was to face the enemy. Yet I had wanted to be beside Julius. By morning I craved sleep, yet I could no more sleep than I could turn and run.

The day drew on and the sun began to penetrate the blanket above us. A winter warmth. Flames licked my stomach and throat and mouth. My bowels felt loose and I trembled inwardly, feeling dread so hot I thought I would faint.

Too soon and the enemy were in sight.

A boy, a girl, and a soldier. We rode upon camels, alone on the plain, toward the Persian army. We were three; they a hundred thousand or more. So littered with tents, the lands before us were a dirty streak on the horizon. I thought of being flayed alive and shivered; pondered whether it truly was too late to turn back as my camel led me inexorably onward.

Men on horseback emerged from the distant camp.

Zenobia held her head high, a sudden chill breeze causing her eyes to narrow as we watched our enemy approach. I touched the hilt of my sword, mirroring Zabbai, felt the weakness of my grip and knew the fear of not being able to hold the iron.

The party that greeted us was not small; a dozen or so. It was too late to turn back now. We were at their mercy. The future was beyond our control. We had no choice but to submit.

We stopped, and the group fanned out around us, moving, never pausing, constantly unnerving. They wore none of their encompassing armour, but thin silk shirts, and more about their face keeping dust from hostile eyes. I stared back, my face set defiant, knowing better than to show the fear churning my stomach.

'Sapor?' Zenobia demanded. Of all the tongues she could speak fluently, Persian was not one of them, but she said the word with confidence.

One man rode close to her. The others watched, their eyes amused, their posture low and yet more menacing for it. The Persian raked Zenobia with his gaze. She wore a thick cloak against the cold, yet the dark skin of her calves showed beneath her silks and fleeces, revealing a hint of what lay beneath.

After a few moments the Persian shouted something to the men behind him, who laughed, then he whooped in turn.

Zabbai half drew his sword, the blade hissing with the promise of death and a lifetime of skill. The laughter ceased. A tense anticipation overcame me as the leader moved across and pulled down the silks covering his face. He was young and with that youth came arrogance. His wiry beard twitched and a snarl appeared as he regarded Zabbai. He drew his own sword, looked about to press it to Zabbai's throat, but he turned to Zenobia. I tensed, heart racing and thumping and tight. He held the point a finger's breadth from her face. His horse stamped in agitation, but the blade did not waver. Zenobia did not move. Her expression remained as impassive, the steel caressing her cheek.

'Sapor,' she said again.

Her voice carried on the silence of the plain, air ringing clear until only an echo of the word remained. She held out her hand to me. I looked back, a moment of confusion, then retrieved the message I had stowed in the saddlebag. I handed it to her and she took it, her eyes fixed on the man who held cold metal to her cheek as she pressed it upon him, lips tight, no trace of fear to be found.

The Persian's expression darkened, but he did not take the scroll immediately. Finally, he snatched the emperor's words from her hand and offered it to another man, who urged his horse forward and accepted it. He prized open the seal and scanned the text before handing it back.

They muttered between them, words low and in their foreign tongue.

Sweat dripped down the side of my face.

Zenobia caught my eye but looked away again, expression fixed. Zabbai glowered at the men surrounding us, face hard and without amusement, a challenge in itself.

Orders relayed between the Persians. Disagreement and hostile words. Then the leader of their group seemed to have his way and the others fell silent.

He bowed slightly, spread his arm, palm up, in mock gesture. I urged my camel on. The Persian horsemen positioned at our rear and flanking, their leader in front.

'What did you say to them?' I asked Zenobia.

'Shapur. Just his name. They knew the scroll was from the

emperor. The leader was afraid that if he killed us, his king would know. He did not wish to risk the wrong decision.'

'And if his king does not wish to see us when we arrive, he will kill us anyway,' I said.

A Persian hissed and no more was said.

A few moments and the enemy camp grew clear, emerging from the sand, distinct and sharp and more terrifying than I could have imagined. And then we were amongst them, surrounded by their dirty, bearded faces, and my heart beat a fast rhythm. This was never a fair fight or a test of skill. Zabbai strode by my side but no general could save us now. Perhaps not even words, even if they were those of a woman, could see us safely home. This was suicide, and I could see no way to survive. I saw only red. Crimson, weeping flesh, stripped and torn from men, their screams loud in my ears, the cries of messengers that Odenathus himself had sent here, and the skies shaking with pain. I had seen one man; bones and muscle and sinew drying in desert heat, eyes staring up from lidless sockets, teeth rotting in a lipless mouth. Bile had risen in my throat at the sight. And I had seen it many times since, nothing could block the vision of it from my mind, and it would never leave me.

I took in the sight of the Persian camp, swallowed; cursed our being here. It was vast. I had seen it only at a distance before: far-off specks of firelight on another shore, in a distant land, a land that had once been ours but far enough from me not to inspire the fear I felt in these moments. Now, surrounded by it, walking into the heart of the enemy, I felt swamped by a tide of dangerous water much larger than the small pool our own army had become.

The camp went about its business, the warriors repairing armour, cooking food, brawling and talking and taking little notice of three strangers hidden amidst a group of their own warriors. Then we came to a large tent near the centre of the camp, its colours far brighter than those around it, taller than most, larger than any other.

The leader of the group raised a hand, gesturing for us to stop. He spoke a few words to his companions, and entered the tent.

We waited.

An age passed, time slow, as if it were not moving at all. Zenobia's face grew hard and irritable, until the man finally reappeared. He spoke to his comrades in their foreign tongue, but it did not hide the crispness, the annoyance, in his tone.

His men ushered us into a smaller tent to the right of the larger one, bare inside, only a faint light penetrating the darkness.

Zenobia edged toward the entrance and parted the opening to see beyond.

'What do you see?' Zabbai asked.

'I can see little,' she murmured. 'There are guards.'

'How long do you think they intend to keep us in here?' The enclosed space filled me with uncertainty, the cramped darkness prickling sweat.

She shrugged, as if it did not matter, as if she could not care. 'For as long as it takes Shapur to have the scroll translated.'

For a heartbeat I forgot the scroll, before recalling that Zenobia had handed it to the Persian warrior. I wondered myself what it said, what words the emperor had written to the king of the Persians, and the bargain he attempted to strike. We were there to find peace, another mission to secure the safety of our country, only this time we were at the mercy of Shapur and not Rome. This time we faced our enemy and not our friends, and this time we could only hope that they would agree to peace, whereas before I had expected only rejection when we sought reinforcements.

We sat for hours, until the sun began to fade and the tent took on a cold gloom. No food or water was brought to us. Our camels had been taken upon our entering the camp, containing all our supplies. And yet Zenobia appeared, as always, unconcerned. She did not speak, nor did she complain. She sat as serene as the goddess Selene, the whites of her eyes and the white of her teeth glowing in the darkness. Her back straight, her chin high, her eyes half-closed.

I felt only apprehension and dread.

Darkness fell entirely and we could no longer make out one another's forms. Only then were the tent flaps flung open, and we were flooded in bright yellow light. I squinted, struggling to see the person holding the torch, a voice barking a command in Persian.

We rose to our feet and followed the figure with the torch whose voice had been so coarse and deep. Outside the tent darkness had not quite consumed all. Men still roamed between tents. Campfires were lit with more warriors huddled around, and women and children too.

A sickly feeling came over me as I heard the Syrian tongue. I turned quickly, searching for the source, as if the familiarity of the sounds would save us.

But I saw women and children chained together. Their faces and limbs were broken and bloody. They crouched in the dirt. One woman stroked a boy's hair with fingers cracked and bent. I looked past the blood and thought the boy a little like Bamdad. His family? Had they survived the fall of Antioch for this? To find themselves in chains? I paused, wanting to approach and ask, to know if they were indeed his family, his wife and children, but I was pushed on.

We headed for the large tent. I trembled with nervousness, struggling to breathe, not knowing if any words would see us leave alive. Zabbai walked beside me, his expression grim.

Zenobia ascended the steps onto the platform first. It set the tent higher than all the rest, higher than an elephant. She did not look back. She did not shake or show any sign that she was afraid. She simply walked into vast tent and I followed.

CHAPTER 8

Zabdas – 290 AD (Present day)

WE PASS RIVERSIDE TOWNS and villages as we journey as far as we can by boat, onward to Hama. A few places I have seen before; recognised from years ago, but others I do not. It is peaceful, even though I know this is my last mission, that I must deliver Jadhima's fate in Rome. This is the journey that I have always been destined to make, no matter what has gone before and in between.

I have family with me. Those I have known in recent years: Samira, Bamdad, even Rostram and the hardness that has taken and consumed him. Only we soldiers know the fate which befell him those long years past. Only I know why he took to a slave ship and this life on the river.

Sadness hangs as I think of those who are dead and gone. I have seen old men perish and I have seen young men die. I have watched children taken by illness and men fall on the edge of a blade. I think of Samira's father, Vaballathus; my son-in-law. I think of him most. Of his dying in my arms, his life taken by Jadhima, King of the Tanukh, as we searched for our own revenge. Yet as Vaballathus' life bled out on the sands, staining the earth a deep red, I took Jadhima and then I sought nothing. I cannot now let death consume me, as it has done before. I took Jadhima's life as if he were a piece of fruit and I sliced his head from his neck and it was done. Finally, he was dead, and at last I had fulfilled every promise I had ever made. Except this last one: to deliver news of the Tanukh king's fate.

The riverbank drifts by, the river named after grandeur, yet I see nothing grand. I see little houses built far enough away that they will not flood if the banks swell, protected by sandbanks, ready to be washed away and rebuilt. And I see the sides of the valley, rocky and grey.

I wonder how different life would have been, how much of the decimation of the east would not have occurred if I had never come to Palmyra as a boy. But I know that nothing would have been different. How could it have been? I was just a boy turned soldier turned general. The struggle between Rome and the Persians would have continued, and Syria was sure to be quashed by it, or to surface above, and with Zenobia ever present, the country would rise.

And if I had not come, if Julius had never found me at the docks of Yemen, I would have still been a slave. An old slave. Dead now after a lifetime of toiling in desert heat, worked to the bone, tired beyond my years. I would never have known the beautiful city that was Palmyra. I would never have known the love of a father, or experienced what it was like to have a family again. Never fought in the ranks of our Bedouin warriors, and not known the sights and the smells and fears and the joy I have experienced. I would never have had my beautiful baby girl and granddaughter in turn. I would not be telling this story.

I watch froth covered ripples float by, looking beyond into the deep murky green of the river. I will continue to tell Samira everything she is required to know, everything I have promised.

She stands on the deck looking out, and I know she is trying to envisage my life. I can taste it at times, in certain foods, in the air and the grit in my food. Or I smell it; the sudden scent on another that so reminds me of Julius, Zenobia, Aurelia and a thousand others I brushed against in my youth, and the perfumed oils familiar to each of them.

Every time I see a girl with golden hair I feel a jolt, a reminder

Zabdas - 290 AD (Present day)

of the young woman who gave herself so wholly to me. For every man with proud posture and hair slicked smooth back with oil, I am teased with memories of the man I came to know as my father, of Julius. Sometimes I see Zenobia in a village, a market place, on her knees in a temple praying to Selene or to Bel. I walk up to her and lay a hand upon her shoulder, say her name, just a whisper on the warm air, bringing her to life. But then she turns and I find it is not her, and the illusion breaks. I dream, too. Real, vivid dreams of a life past or the impression of a day that never truly occurred, then I wake. But I force myself to close my eyes and continue the dream, knowing it is not true, and that I can never live those years again.

It is easier amongst friends. Beside Bamdad and with Samira and those familiar to me, especially now Vaballathus is gone. They distract me from my thoughts, even though our mission is always on my mind, pushing me forwards, carving into the future what is meant to be.

I see what must be done, and it is an easy task; not physically enduring. Still I know there is an element of closure in my written words. Parting with the story of Zenobia is as if I am free of it. Free of what happened.

Bamdad approaches. His eyes are hard. He is angry with me.

'Why in the name of the fucking gods have you told Samira about me?'

I smile. I cannot help it. Bamdad is angry but he is only angry because he is a part of the story, part of the history of these lands, and he is afraid of what I might tell Samira, who looks up to him as she looks up to me. She is fond of him, and he is concerned he might lose that.

'You were there,' I say. 'You know what happened. What I have told her.'

'You will tell her everything, then?'

I do not answer. Bamdad knows much, but not all. My eyes ache and I rub them and take a deep breath. I stretch to the sky, tiredness taking hold, my limbs stiff and my mind dulled by a busy day aboard the boat.

'I will tell her everything. She should know.'

'If you must, make sure you are kind to me,' he says. 'Don't make me look like a fool.' He strides away.

I look back at Apamea, almost lost from view, a small blur on a fading horizon. The towns and villages are sparse the further we travel. I feel eyes upon us, watching our every move, even in this desolate place. I am unnerved. There is something out there. I could say it is the scavenging nomad tribes that induce my paranoia, but I know it is not. There is a price on my head; the man who killed the king of the Tanukh.

A soldier keeps a keen eye on the horizon, for there is always an enemy, always a revenge to exact, a man wanting to draw blood. I had thought us safe, away from Palmyra, a small company, but I know that we are not.

There was a time, many years ago, when I did not feel threat from those people I call my own, my countrymen; my brothers. We were warriors feared by our enemies, respected by the citizens of Syria.

I look to the riverbank either side of the boat and up at the steep slopes of the valley, and see a glimmer, the sort of light that metal might reflect. The kind I use to send signals when preparing for battle. And I know then that someone else is out there watching, waiting. I could call them out and stand my ground, hunt them as they hunt us, for I am not afraid, but I cannot fight what I could not see, and I would rather move on, head for Rome, and leave them far behind.

Samira sits with my men on the bow of the boat, watches them struggle to fight one another, training as they have done all their lives; even now, when no army exists in this barren land but for the men I left in Palmyra. These men aboard ship were once warriors, the elite of the Bedouin, men who had seen more war than sand.

Zabdas - 290 AD (Present day)

Rostram, how I remember him, a warrior I have known almost his whole life. He is perhaps thirty-five years now, age and battle not as apparent on his flesh. He duels with Kairash, his friend. Kairash wields two blades of curved steel, catching the light with each movement, knowing that he will not beat Rostram, for Rostram is arrogant and rightly so. He is one of the strongest, quickest, most favoured warriors I have known. He moves much faster than Kairash, slipping and sliding along the deck, avoiding the blades, chuckling with grim certainty. He turns and cuts, turns and cuts again, slicing and whistling with his own two blades, and all the while Kairash parries with brute strength.

'Rostram will win.'

I sit next to Samira. She is watching them, intrigued by the training which yields itself to another grudge match between two old friends.

'He has won twice already,' she admits as blades ring and the dozen men of the crew shout encouragement, willing them both on, not caring who wins, spoiling only for a good fight.

'That is why no bets are taken,' I say.

Samira appears thoughtful. She has not taken her eyes from Rostram. But then she says: 'When Zenobia lost her child and she lay close to death, did you really believe she would die?'

I consider for a moment. 'If I am honest, no, I did not. I feared she would, but I cannot say that I ever truly thought she would die. She was strong, much stronger than anyone I have known. Her will was greater than most. But at the time I was young, I was selfish, and I was afraid.'

'You admit a great deal,' she says. 'You tell me this story, and everything of your youth.'

For a moment I do not know what to say. I anticipate questions, but not comment on my character. What I did then, perhaps, but not who I am now.

'Perhaps I do,' I say, but I am unsure. Do I admit a lot? I had thought to recount a tale, and one of someone other than myself.

'And Mareades,' she says. 'I cannot believe his betrayal, nor that Zenobia could forgive him. Thousands died because of him.'

I see then the hardness in Samira. A young girl who would judge; a girl sure enough of her own mind to draw conclusions.

'She never forgave him. She simply understood the path he chose, that is all. She was right, I realised later. She knew that the worst thing he could lose was his pride. I believe she understood him better than anyone. She understood us all.'

'You said she had bruising, to her face. Was it the king? Was it Odenathus?'

'I admit, that was my first thought. But it was not Odenathus. Valerian struck her, for her charity toward Mareades and for the subsequent fall of Antioch. Once Bamdad and I left, Odenathus and Valerian argued, Zenobia too, and in his anger and frustration he hit her. He was a coward, lashing his anger to the only person in the room he reasonably could. He ought to have blamed himself for the predicament in which he found himself; the loss of the great eastern cities and the plague depleting his troops, but he did not. Instead he blamed everyone else. It was easy, for he was an emperor, and none dared to stand against him. Even his own men, those sworn to his service, began to murmur their discontent.'

'What happened? What did Odenathus do?'

'He did nothing. He ignored it as if it had not happened. You must remember that his position was a delicate one. He held only a small amount of authority whilst Valerian remained in the east, and that could be taken away at any moment.'

Bamdad joins the men watching Rostram and Kairash. I see him exchange coins, betting on the outcome. Fool, I think. Nothing has changed. He bets now as has always done; recklessly and without regard.

'What of Bamdad?' Samira asks. 'Did he ever find his wife, his children? Did he come to know of their fate?'

I looked across at Bamdad, his grin cheeky, of our history that has changed him. He will not show it, not on the surface,

Zabdas - 290 AD (Present day)

but beneath I know him to be a different man.

'He never found them. Presumed them taken as slaves to the Persian capital, to Ctesiphon. He found another wife not long after.' Not long, I say again, this time to myself. It was not immediate, not a day or a week or a month after, but a short while. This was his way of moving on, forgetting the pain of their loss which must have haunted him.

'Did not Haddudan, the priest king, pay for the lies he told? The lies which saw Mareades branded a slave and the justice the senator of Antioch felt he was owed; the reason for his betrayal?'

'Haddudan fled to the mountains with as much gold as he and his camel could carry. His lies were not punished for a long time.'

Rostram parries a hefty blow from Kairash. Both men are sweating, neither willing to give up, despite heavy limbs and small scratches beading with blood which must sting. They continue to dance around one other; Rostram light on his feet, his hair slick with oil and composed concentration on his face. Kairash circles with lumbering steps, bringing his sword down and across in heavy arcs. I would not wish to know the bludgeoning his blade can deliver, the force with which he defeats opponents.

Rostram grins to his friend, side-steps a blow, drives the butt of his sword into Kairash's gut. Onlookers cheer and coin begins to change hands. But Kairash recovers and returns the blow, this time catching Rostram off-guard. Rostram drops his sword and clutches his stomach, keels in pain, face glowing red with embarrassment.

Kairash offers his hand. Rostram takes it and laughs. And I see Bamdad grin for the wager he has won.

'Rostram is not angry,' Samira says, almost to herself.

'He is good-humoured,' I reply. 'And they have been friends for a long time. It is not often Kairash can beat him. They know one another too well, you see. They know one another's tricks and steps, how the other moves and holds their sword. Fighting a man you have never faced before is much different.'

I stretch and stand up, my limbs not as supple as they once were, my muscles tight, still suffering from the encounter on the slave ship. Men whom I had never faced before, whose blades were new to me and whose lives I had taken.

'I have written more of the tale of Zenobia. I may write a little more today. You can read it if you wish.'

'Of course!'

I look at the waters, bright and reflective and calm. It is as if they are calling to me, their depth and the darkness below the surface bringing warning.

I kiss Samira's forehead and put an arm about her shoulders, pulling her toward me, as we move below deck to where I write.

'You walked into the Persian camp?' Samira's face is slack with astonishment. She sits beside me as I write, turning parchment, eager to know what will become of our mission to gain audience with Shapur.

'We did,' I say.

'And Zenobia was not afraid?'

'She must have felt fear, but she did not show it. She could not risk revealing weakness to our enemy.'

'I cannot understand. Why did the emperor attempt to sue for peace? Why did he send you and Zenobia and Zabbai to certain danger?' she asks.

I look at the words I scrawled on the parchment a moment before. *Fate is inexorable.*

'Because we were meant to go. Valerian was a desperate man. Plague hitting the troops a final blow. Our defences were depleted, and from what I saw within the Persian camp, they were not suffering as we did. Plague had yet to poison their ranks, whereas the morale of our soldiers had plummeted.

'You must remember that Emperor Valerian only secured his position through the usurpation of his predecessor. It had happened so many times during the reign of Gallienus that those making claim, or assumed to be attempting to make claim, became known as the Thirty Tyrants. Valerian must have worried that attempts would be made for his throne, a likely candidate then being Odenathus. He was a great leader, having held the Persians at bay for many years, and he knew the love of his people. It was why Valerian kept Odenathus' control in the east to a minimum. And perhaps Valerian was right; our only chance of survival would be to agree a peace of sorts.

'Years before, even before I had come to Syria, Odenathus made attempt to contact Shapur, because he wanted peace and he knew that peace with Shapur would mean better trade and safer roads. Every messenger had been returned dead. Valerian's intentions were confused, even in his own mind, I suspect. He saw peace as his only choice, but he also wanted to punish Odenathus whilst ridding him of Zenobia's influence. Perhaps he did believe Zenobia stood a better chance at gaining an audience with Shapur than anyone else. She was a woman, after all, high-born and with status. He might genuinely have believed the Persians would not harm a queen and a woman, because in Rome they would not. But I did not believe it for a heartbeat.'

I scratch my bearded chin and look back at the words on the parchment. They are blurred. My eyes are not what they used to be and they are tired.

'The emperor was a fool,' Samira says.

'And a coward.'

'An insufferable man who could not ...' She laughs. 'This is what Bamdad would say.'

I laugh too. 'He would. And Valerian was all of those things. But he was our emperor, and so we did as we were ordered. We went into the very heart of the enemy camp ...'

'Did Zenobia have a plan? Did she know what would happen?' Samira is intrigued, I think, by the woman who willingly walked into the Persian lair. Who proclaimed to be descended from the gods. And who can blame her?

'Ah, you ask an interesting question, Samira. Zenobia always had ideas forming in her mind. She appeared willing to meet with Shapur, when in reality we had no choice. Odenathus could not have stopped Valerian sending us. We could have deserted, of course, but to where? Zenobia could not come back a queen if she ran. And it is not something she would ever have contemplated. We cared too much for Syria not to take the chance to save it. Zenobia was so driven she would stop at nothing.'

'And yet Odenathus did not even see Zenobia leave. He was not there at the gates as you rode to meet with Shapur. What if she did not return?'

'The relationship between Odenathus and Zenobia was always strained, right from the first, when Julius bargained his services for his daughter's voice on the Palmyrene council. And then Zenobia lost Odenathus' child. I believe at that moment he was overcome with grief. He could not bear to watch her go. Could not speak to her or find words as she parted. Or it could have been she asked him not to bid farewell. It could have been her who did not want him there. In addition, his position amongst the Roman generals controlling his troops in Syria hampered him. Valerian would not allow Odenathus to make decisions alone, so for all the threats Valerian made of stripping him of the title 'king', it would have made no difference if he had. It struck Odenathus, I think, to feel the power he held snatched from him by the very people he loyally served, knowing all the while it was not for the greater good. And of course Zenobia had saved Mareades for me and in the king's name, and it became the catastrophe that lost Antioch, making Odenathus' position worse still.'

I put my reed pen to papyrus once more. I have had many years to ponder the actions of men, to understand their decisions and what may or may not have been the right course on any given day, in a situation that few could ever understand. Perhaps I have always been too close to see the reality of the people in my past.

CHAPTER 9

Zabdas – 260 AD

WE FOLLOWED THE GUARD into the tent. A great bath made of gold sat on golden feet, partly hidden behind swathes of patterned fabric of reds and greens and deep, rich yellow. Around us, more cloth hung from ceiling and the walls, tied back and draping like a river of water, the finest of the orient, rich in colour and delicate of weave. Almost everything was made of gold: before us a low table of yellow presented cups of gold and of silver. Fine carpets adorned the floor, golden threads shimmering in pale afternoon light. Jewels lay everywhere; on the table, the floor, hanging from the roof, hanging from walls and sewn into the curtains. This tent was designed to impress those granted audience, to show the wealth and power of Persia, and I wondered if the only reason we had not yet been slaughtered was to witness and marvel it.

But I also knew that every item had once belonged to men of Syria, and suddenly the bright reflections dulled somewhat, and the whole room sank into a dimness I could not suppress. The muscles in my face set firm in my disgust.

Upon the low table our scroll had been placed. Waiting. The reason we had come. I looked past the table to a throne behind. A figure sat, camouflaged amidst those fabrics and riches all about. More jewels hung upon the man: woven into his hair, sewn upon his clothes, lacing his hands and I wondered how he might move his fingers. His face twitched at the sight of us, a thin, dark beard and moustache hiding what remained of a face already layered with yet more jewels. From a band across his forehead and from his ears and his nose hung red, green, amber, purple and misty grey stones.

Either side of the man stood two guards, muscular forms proud, the wall behind us holding their gaze. Another, younger man, stood to the right of the throne. He swallowed hard, wrung his hands continuously, his expression one of fear and of terror. His dirty old clothes were out of place amongst the wealth of the tent.

No one spoke. I stared at the man upon the throne, and he looked back at us through narrow eyes. His wiry beard twitched; the only sign of life in a rigid form. Eventually, following a long, uncomfortable silence, Zenobia spoke.

'Shapur?' she demanded, her voice unwavering, her expression hard.

The great figure narrowed his eyes further, irritation flickering. He turned his head only slightly and addressed the young man beside him. He spoke in the Persian tongue and the young man, his eyes downturned, nodded rapidly before looking directly at Zabbai.

'Shapur I the Great, King of Kings, Son of a King, Son of Ardashir, Ruler of the Sassanian Empire, wishes to know who dares to enter his camp.' The titles were mighty, and yet the man's voice trembled, his whole being visibly shaking as he spoke in Syrian, his dialect that of the north; Antioch or Apamea.

Before Zabbai could respond, Zenobia, her gaze fixed and her voice calm, said: 'Tell your king that he addresses Zenobia, Queen of Palmyra, wife of King Odenathus and Illustrious Consul our Lord, Consul of Rome.'

Shapur spoke again to his translator.

'My king asks who accompanies you.'

'It is irrelevant,' she replied. 'I am here to speak with King Shapur, nothing more.'

The translator's eyes were once again diverted to the floor. I looked to each person in the room in turn, waiting for someone to speak, for Zenobia to continue or for Shapur to respond, for his translator to say something more.

Finally, Shapur murmured once more.

'The King of Persia wishes to know why the King of Palmyra sends his wife with messages on his behalf. He wonders why King Odenathus does not value the life of his queen. Why he sends only two soldiers to accompany you into enemy territory. Why he does not send a man?'

'My life is my own,' Zenobia replied. 'I do with it as I wish. Tell your king I appreciate his concern for my wellbeing.'

She smiled a little, and Shapur's expression seemed to shift with puzzlement, his darting eyes beckoning his interpreter to tell him what had been said. He recognised some of our words, it seemed, but not all.

When the translator had finished, his expression grew harder, his eyes narrower, before he barked out a gruff, humourless laugh.

I looked to Zabbai to find him as worried as I. His face was cold and set, but a shift of weight from one foot to another betrayed him. Zenobia remained smiling, as if sharing Shapur's amusement.

Shapur murmured again, the jewels upon his face chinking slightly, his eyes never leaving us, the gold surrounding him reflecting every movement.

'My King of Kings says you amuse him with your forthrightness. He says that if a wife of his spoke in such a way, he would show her to whom her life belonged. He would ensure that she did not forget.' The translator finished speaking, but Shapur seemed to know he had not repeated everything, and flicked his hand aggressively for the young man to continue. The translator stammered and looked to the floor. 'He says he would cut her hands from her arms, he would cut her feet from her legs. He would carve out her eyes and slice from her body her breasts.

He would cut open her stomach and pull from it every organ required to live. And with these parts he would feed his dogs. That way the dogs would have her life, and he would have given it to them.'

My stomach turned and swam. I felt hot with sweat and the incense in the room, which I had not noticed before now, suddenly overwhelmed. I begged wordlessly for Zenobia not to antagonise the Persian king, but she smiled back at him, apparently unconcerned.

'Is that why you have so many wives?' Zenobia asked.

Shapur did not smile. He did not laugh. He showed no sign of displeasure or otherwise as the interpreter relayed her words. When the young man had finished, he muttered a rapid response.

'My King of Kings, Ruler of the Sasanian Empire, has many wives because he likes women. He says he would like you, if you were untouched, if you had not been taken by a Syrian, a Roman, because he knows no woman that dares to stand in front of him as you do now, without fear. He asks if King Odenathus has only one wife.'

'He has only one. Only I am welcome in Odenathus' bed,' Zenobia replied.

'There was one before you?'

'Only one, and she is dead.'

'My king assumes she was submissive, as a wife. That you are nothing like her. That she obeyed her king, did not assume equal rank, that he bedded many women when with her. That he had a harem.'

'I never met King Odenathus' first wife,' Zenobia replied. 'And I know of no harem. Odenathus does not follow your example. And as much as I would gladly discuss the position of wives and the expectation of them, I am not here for that. I am to give you a message.' She gestured to the scroll on the golden table. 'I bring word from Valerian Caesar, Emperor of the Roman Empire.'

Again Zenobia's words were passed between the king and

his interpreter. Shapur made several motions toward the scroll. When they had finished, Shapur turned back to us and the interpreter looked up once more.

'My king has read the scroll in the emperor's Latin words, and he asks why he should agree to peace when he has already defeated you?'

'We are not defeated. Our army is equal in number to yours,' Zenobia lied. 'You face the armies of both Syria and Rome. We have men from Germania, Thrace, Pamphylia, Lycaonia, Galatia, Lycia, Cilicia, Cappodocia, Mauritania, Judea, Rhodes, Mesopotamia, Rome and Syria. The might of the Empire is behind us. Continue if you wish, but you will perish at the hands of our armies. We come now to secure peace. We do not wish more men to die. We do not desire death for your people. Peace is your only option if you wish to return to Persia with the riches you have.'

The translator struggled to keep up with Zenobia. When she finished speaking, when the echo of her words died on the fabric of the tent, when the translator uttered the last of her words in Persian, Shapur's retort deafened. The interpreter dropped to his knees, cowering, the guards flinched and seemed to recoil from the King of Kings, the might that was Shapur.

'I have faced your emperors before,' he bellowed. 'On the border of Babylonia and Misikhe, there was a great battle; greater than any of this.' He swung his arm as if to encompass our two forces, of the men we had and his own, and of the country he ravaged. 'And there I killed Gordian Caesar. Then Marcus Julius Philippus Augustus came to me for terms, just as you do now, but he ransomed his life and that of his men for 500,000 denars; a better man than *your* emperor. But Caesar lied again and wronged me, and so I *attacked* the Roman Empire and annihilated 60,000 strong Roman and Syrian forces. We burned, pillaged and ruined Syria, just as we do now. We conquered Sura, Barbalissos, Zeugma, Urima, Gindaros, Armenaza, Seleucia, Antioch, Cyrrhe and many, many more.

'Valerian Caesar asks to meet. Writes of gifting to me your beloved city of Palmyra if I take nothing more. Does he not understand me? I care nothing for cities, I care only for what they contain. And I can take that with or without his consent. Does your emperor think to cow me, Palmyrene Queen? Does he really think it is enough? That I will grovel to accept his offer? That a city of marble will suffice?'

The translator breathed deeply in this pause, quivering, still kneeling upon the floor, tears streaming down his face.

My own face must have dropped. The revelation of Valerian's proposal to sacrifice Palmyra, the wealthiest of Syrian cities; our home, shocked. I could not believe the words, that this is what the scroll contained, and that we ourselves had been demanded to deliver it. How ironic, I thought. How spiteful of Valerian. The coward, the liar, a weak man in a purple cloak. He did not deserve to wear the colour.

Shapur's eyes bore into Zenobia's, and I glanced to her. She did not flinch. She gave no indication of knowing Valerian's intention, or surprise at the discovery.

Shapur went on: 'I can take Palmyra, just as I have conquered Antioch and many of your cities. Odenathus has already attempted to sue for peace many times. He has sent one man after another, knowing that I would not agree. I sent his messengers back with my reply.'

'You sent them back flayed,' Zenobia replied, her tone matter of fact, her voice a little raised.

'What makes you think I will not send you back the same? Red flesh of a queen, stripped bare of skin for all to see?' the translator repeated, speaking to the carpet upon which he still knelt.

'I have more to offer you than a mere half-million denars; more than the city of Palmyra.' Zenobia took a step closer, her shoulders square, her mouth amused, her hands palm up, presenting her next words.

The two guards standing either side of Shapur moved forward, but Shapur stilled them with a hand.

'You cannot offer me your body, Palmyrene Queen. Your cunt does not interest me. You are beautiful, more beautiful than most. And yet I have exquisite women in my harem to rival your looks. You might outmatch them, you might think yourself their superior. You might think quickly and be more knowledgeable that many men. Yes, you might be all of these things, but you cannot think I would exchange peace with Rome for your virtue, even if you are a queen? Is that why I was sent a woman, to tempt me? To soften me? The Roman Emperor thinks I am fool enough to be weakened by you?' As he spoke, Shapur's face barely moved, nothing except a small quiver of his mouth indicating it was from him the Persian words came.

'You are wrong,' Zenobia replied. 'I was not sent to tempt you ...'

Shapur stilled her talking with his hand. The conversation progressed so rapidly the translator could no longer keep pace with their exchange. Once he had caught up, Shapur rested his hand back upon the arm of his throne, his jewelled fingers caressing it. His face perhaps betraying mild amusement.

Even then, once the translator had finished, he said nothing and neither did Zenobia speak. Then he said: 'Why have you come to my camp? What do you think you have that will secure peace? You have gold and riches, but I have taken much of those already, and I will take the rest. Your lands have been raped by my army. What have you that I cannot take for myself?'

'The Emperor of Rome.'

She spoke with no trace of a smile, nor a hint of tone in her voice. She said the words as clearly as I heard Julius tell me that Meskenit was my mother. It was as if all sound had stopped, that no soldier moved beyond the tent in which we stood. The whole world stopped, and the gods watched without breath.

I met Zabbai's eye, searching for clarification, eager to know of what had been said. But there was no explanation to be found, no reassurance, no betrayed understanding.

Zenobia said nothing more. After a long pause, Shapur muttered to his guards in his Persian tongue. In silence they moved behind us. They lifted chairs from the wall of the tent and placed them down, indicating we should sit.

Shapur leaned forward in his throne, his frame larger as his shoulders curled, and looked deep into Zenobia's eyes. He rubbed his bearded chin, and sat back in his chair, taking in the three of us.

'You wish to give me the Emperor of Rome?' The interpreter remained kneeling as he continued to translate the king's words. 'Why?'

'Why is not important. I will deliver him. You can do with him as you wish. His life is of no concern to me. In return, you leave Syria indefinitely. You do not return. You do not harry our borders. You leave us in peace. Never again shall you place foot on Syrian sand.'

'The ransom of an emperor will not amount to the plunder I can gain in your lands.'

Zenobia shifted next to me until she too was leaning forward on her chair. 'Perhaps not,' she conceded. 'But would you want an emperor's ransom? I would not. I can think of a far greater pleasure to be had than coin. Never before has an emperor of Rome been taken captive by an enemy. You would write history; one of the Persian Empire's greatest victories over the Roman Empire. *Your* name gracing the pages of *our* literature. You would be a fool not to agree to the arrangement.'

'I have my own people, my own literature, and I have no need of proving anything to your people.'

Zenobia sat back in the chair. Shapur regarded us with interest.

'Your companions, they knew nothing of this proposition?'

'They did not, no. But then I think they did not foresee Emperor Valerian's betrayal of our city.'

Zenobia looked at each of us in turn, the surety of her features putting aside any doubt I had that her plan was the right one. Zabbai gave a reluctant nod of consent as she turned back to Shapur. She did not need our approval. Nor did she need our support. She had not told us what she planned to say to the Persian king once there, this man before us, this round hulk of beast, a king of kings. Perhaps I should have felt betrayed that she had not confided in Zabbai and me, but there was a glimmer of hope in that moment, because there was a chance we could leave alive.

'If you take prisoner Emperor Valerian, with or without my assistance, it will be the most humiliating moment in Roman history. You will be remembered as the man who captured a Caesar. Your enemies will fear you for it. Your people will love you.'

Shapur looked upon us differently as he took in her words. I could see him imagining taking the emperor back to Ctesiphon and parading him in the Persian capital for his people, dragging him through the dusty streets, humiliating him. He must have known it would unify his own troops, that his cause would be solidified and that more would be willing to join his ranks for the plunder it would bring. I watched as the idea took hold of him, until his eyes glazed, his sight wandered, and I knew he could no longer concentrate on conversing with Zenobia. Perhaps he thought of his achievements becoming greater than those of his father, Ardashir. Or perhaps he thought of his empire becoming the greatest in the world.

He muttered to the interpreter.

'You must stay in the camp tonight. Tomorrow, I will give you my decision. Either way, you will be sent back to your King Odenathus with a message. If I decide you are attempting to fool me, your bodies will be returned.'

'As you wish,' Zenobia responded, dipping her head in acknowledgment.

Zabbai and I did the same.

He spoke again and gestured to the scroll still lying on the table.

'If you had come to me with this pitiful offer written here alone, I would have killed you already.'

I had thought for a moment, a heartbeat, that our lives were assured. That the king of the Persians would consider Zenobia's words, her idea plausible. But his last words did not leave me as the guards ushered us from the Shapur's presence.

Outside the camp moved as before; the soldiers' noise had not ceased, they had not heard the words exchanged between Shapur and Zenobia, what had passed between their leader and us.

'Odenathus knows nothing of what you have offered Shapur?' I said, my energy drained, my heart weak and without hope. If Shapur agreed, who knew what it would mean when we returned home?

'Do not speak of it now,' Zenobia snapped.

We followed the guards back to the tent in which we had spent much of the day waiting. Zenobia settled on the cushions that had been scattered upon the floor during our absence. Zabbai and I remained standing.

'Does he know?' Zabbai demanded of her. I would have asked myself, but Zabbai was as eager to have explanation of what had occurred in Shapur's tent.

'It matters not whether Odenathus knows of any promise or agreement between myself and Shapur. It is done.'

'It can be undone,' Zabbai growled.

'If it is undone, the east falls. We would not leave here alive, you heard as much with your own ears. Our people would perish. And our bodies would have been returned flayed,' she said in a loud voice. Then more quietly: 'Valerian Caesar cares nothing for your life, just as he cares nothing for Zabdas' life or mine. He makes our people suffer. Odenathus has long held our frontier, rewarded by hostility and bitter, futile acts of petty revenge for his position and courage, for the simple fact that he is a threat to the imperium Valerian holds. And yes Odenathus is loyal to the emperor, no matter how much he is despised in return. No matter what that emperor forces our king to do. Do you think we would be here had Odenathus known what I endeavour to achieve?'

'What exactly *do* you wish to achieve?' Zabbai's voice rose and I heard murmurs from outside. With a hushing motion from me, they both dipped their voices.

'With the emperor of Rome gone, the highest rank will take control over the remaining legions. As king, Odenathus would have complete control over the east, and thus we could make a stand to cause Shapur to tremble with fear. With our persuasion, Odenathus would accept the position. He would have no choice. And Gallienus, I think, would be thankful for it.'

Zenobia was fuelled, and I could not help but be reminded of Julius, of his passion, and of his beliefs; that she had gone further than he had ever gone. That she was perhaps mad with her ambition.

She looked at us keenly, her eyes determined that we should understand, begging for our agreement to what she had done. She was afraid, I think. Not of being in the Persian camp, not of Valerian or Odenathus and what they might think, but of whether her aims were true, if they had Syria at their heart; whether her father would agree with her actions.

I could not answer for Julius. Nor could I answer for myself. I was struck with the enormity of what we were doing. Zabbai, however, gave a curt nod.

'I do not agree with everything you have done,' he said, 'or how you have done it. You should *never* have lied to Odenathus. But if we can secure Syria, save our people, and leave here alive, then I am with you.'

'Zabdas?' The faintest hint of pleading in her cool, demanding voice.

'Agreed,' I murmured, my tone empty of emotion, my mind no longer able to ascertain my true thoughts. 'I am with you also. We deliver the emperor as you have promised. But what makes you think Shapur believes you?'

'Why would he think we attempt to trick him? No matter what I say, he knows our numbers have dropped through plague. He knows that we have been beaten over and over by his troops. We are losing; our only chance is to barter with the one thing unattainable to him. Not one emperor, in the history of the Roman Empire, has been taken captive by an enemy. Valerian would flee before that became a possibility. It is the one thing Shapur never thought he could have. He knows that to take an emperor of Rome captive would mean incalculable praise and support from his people, that he will become greater than his predecessors. If he passes on this chance, he will never see it again. He will never know that greatness.'

'And you think Valerian will walk into a trap set by Shapur?' I asked.

She shook her head. 'I think he will walk into a trap set by *us*. Valerian thinks that securing peace is the only way to still the east while he moves his forces back to the Goth invaders. He does not want to do it, and I know Shapur will never agree to a peace treaty from a Roman; he admitted he would not have accepted Palmyra in exchange, you heard that. Even if he did, he would still take the rest of Syria, then Rome, because there is nothing to stop him. Not if Palmyra is taken. We are the strongest city here. Give him that, and we give him everything.'

'It is impossible to believe. That Valerian sent us with a message that gave up our own city!' Zabbai said, and suddenly his voice erupted with anger.

Zenobia frowned. 'I had my suspicions.'

'What happens when the Persians have the emperor and we have our peace? What then?' Zabbai's voice dropped level again, his brow deep with concern as he waited for Zenobia's response. 'What is to stop him pressing further into Syria?'

Zenobia looked at us both. She was adorned with the jewels of a queen; every part of her sure and determined.

'Nothing will stop him. Shapur will never keep to his word,' She dared to smile. 'They will think we retire to our homes in the wake of peace, when in fact we will strike. You forget. We will have the remainder of the Roman army at our disposal. Under the right command, we will have the troops needed to rid Syria of the Persian invaders once and for all.'

Slaves brought bread and ham to our tent and we ate. By morning, my head felt thick with sleeplessness and worry, compounded by the knowledge that we must soon face the Persian king once more, our fate decided by his whim and his greed. Zenobia's features were haughty, eyes rimmed by more than kohl, with tiredness. Still she appeared eager to discover our fate.

I scratched my bearded chin as Zabbai fastened his sword-less belt; our weapons were taken upon entering the camp. None of us spoke. We had exhausted every angle, all possibilities, each outcome, until our mouths were dry and there was nothing left but repetition.

Not long after I heard the camp stir, a messenger came to our tent. He silently signalled for us to move out into the brilliant morning sun. I could see nothing but the blur of men crossing my path, the shadow of the man in front, the white of the sun. And then my eyes adjusted. Once again, we were being led to the great tent; Shapur's tent. The King of Kings. More than a hundred guards, their armour bouncing blinding light, stood at the foot of the platform upon which the tent had been erected. We passed the guards, their swords and bows standing proud, the menace of their presence unmistakeable.

Zabbai shot me a brief look of concern, but still followed Zenobia, who strode confidently into the depths of Shapur's abode.

The Persian king did not move as we entered, his eyes closed as if in sleep. The chairs we had been invited to sit upon the previous day had gone. To his side waited the slave who would translate as he had before.

Shapur opened his eyes and looked at us long and hard, his small, narrow eyes unreadable.

'King Shapur,' Zenobia said, dipping her head in greeting.

The king remained motionless, apart from his lips, which moved rapidly.

'I have considered your proposal carefully,' the translator began. 'How would you ensure the emperor enters the trap? What will you say to convince him to meet?'

'Valerian Caesar is a coward,' Zenobia replied. 'It is why he asked us to come and discuss the peace he wants, to have you back from Syria and his frontier, to persuade you to meet. He is willing to meet with you anyway, but I will make it so. I will ensure he comes with less men than you, I will tell him you are also wanting to make peace, because plague ravages your troops, that I have seen it myself. I will tell him you want Palmyra, and that you feel his proposition is the only way forward, and I will ensure the King Odenathus presses him. I will also advise the ground upon which it will be best to take him as your prisoner. I know these lands well. I will do everything I can to ensure you have him as your prisoner.'

Beneath the jewels hanging from the band on Shapur's forehead, his eyes flickered.

'I agree to your proposal, Palmyrene Queen.'

My heart lifted. The weight of worry somewhat lighter than it had been a moment before. We would leave alive. We would not be flayed for the amusement of this Persian king.

'But assurances are required,' he continued, 'so that you to keep your word. I would not have you leave here alive without them.'

Beside me, Zenobia stiffened in frustration. Clearly she had hoped there would be no terms, no guarantee, that her word would be enough to secure her desires.

'What assurances do you require?' she said.

Shapur lifted a finger slowly and spoke. He pointed directly to me. I knew then my fate.

'No,' Zenobia said flatly before the Shapur's words had been translated. 'Those terms are unacceptable.'

'I will stay behind until Valerian Caesar is taken,' Zabbai interjected.

I looked at him, startled by his gesture, but unable to let him offer himself in my place.

'You cannot,' I uttered.

'Neither.' Her voice quavering with anger, Zenobia met Shapur's small eyes. 'You will take neither. Their lives as assurance was not the offer I made to you.'

Shapur spoke again, his tone full of amusement.

'You are afraid, queen of the east. To be a queen you must sacrifice, at whatever personal cost. You want to rule. You want to broker bargains between Rome and her enemies. I assume you led these men here, and yet you are unwilling to go as far as is necessary to secure the outcome you want so much.' He looked at us for a moment, enjoyment dancing in his features as the interpreter relayed his words. 'You have no choice. Either he stays, or you all die and I will ravage Palmyra just as I have ravaged Antioch and the other cities that you hold dear.'

'Then I shall stay,' Zenobia said, but I realised her worry as the words left her lips. She must be present to ensure that Valerian followed the path, fell into the trap, she could not stay. And I dared not think what would happen if we failed, if Valerian did not come and was not taken captive.

Panic stricken, I gripped her arm. 'No, you cannot.'

Shapur laughed.

'You have confirmed everything I needed to know. I do not accept your offer to stay in his place. Of the three of you, Palmyrene queen, you are the one to ensure Valerian Caesar will come. The one you care for most must stay behind.' He pointed to me.

For the first time I saw Zenobia struggle between necessity and the bond we shared, unable to make the decision. Was I presumptive, I wondered? Did she care for me in a way that I cared for her, with the same care that I had shown as I sat at her bedside as she lay close to death? She had never shown such loss of composure before. She had always been willing to give whatever it took to succeed in her ambition; she had given her whole self to her father's dream. But now I could see her torn, just as I had been torn when leaving Rome and Aurelia. She could not envisage leaving as two, not three.

Almost imperceptibly, I nodded and leaned closer to her, so my cheek brushed hers as I held her arm in a firm grip.

'I trust in you,' I murmured. 'Bring the emperor, secure peace, do whatever you need to. I will remain here and wait for you.'

'And if I cannot bring him? If he will not come?' she hissed; her voice too low for the interpreter to hear and translate. For a moment, brief and unseen by anyone but me, the mask of surety and determination collapsed to reveal a girl, a little older than myself, afraid of losing a friend, her brother, afraid of where her determination and ambition led her; led us.

'When have you ever failed? When have you ever been *afraid* of failure?' I growled. I was angry at her then. That she had begun to collapse. As much as I sometimes wanted to see her weaknesses, to know her fully, to witness what lay beneath her hard exterior, I did not wish to see it now.

She looked down and took my hand in hers. Gripped it hard. I gripped back.

Her cheeks flushed. She turned back to Shapur, all resolution returning.

'I accept your terms. Harm him in any way, and you will have nothing.'

Shapur spoke loudly in his tongue and two guards entered, gripped my upper arms tight, and guided me from the tent.

As I left, Zenobia's voice rang tight with anger. 'You have my assurance, King of the Persians, now I want yours!'

CHAPTER 10

Zabdas – 260 AD

Whatever passed between Shapur and Zenobia once I left I do not know. I was led to a dank cage. Animal faeces coated the floor and urine stained the bars. This was to be our humiliation; that Shapur could do as he desired, that it was us who had sought him, and therefore it was he who held the power, he alone could do as he wished and we could do nothing to stop it.

The door opened and I was pushed in, out of sight, a hostage, my life held in the balance for that of an emperor. Two men stood guard over me as I retched at the inescapable stench and reflected how much my life was worth now. I had once been a slave to a dockside chief, worth only that of a good bookkeeper. Now I was held by the Persian king himself, known as the boy befriended by the queen of the east, her half-brother and confidant, and yet I was judged worthy of the life of an emperor by both Shapur and Zenobia. I was worth what she was willing to exchange to have me back. To Zenobia, I was worth Rome.

Day crawled into night and night back into day. The sun beat down on the cage until the bars were too hot to touch and my thirst became more than I could bear.

The guards brought water, dank and gritty; enough to keep me alive, nothing more. Scraps of food were pushed through the

The Fate of an Emperor

bars, and shame overtook me in the days I sat there, for feeling such gratitude to my captors.

Would my situation become Valerian's fate? Would he see the inside of these bars as I did, hungry and thirsty, afraid of what would become of him? My stomach clenched with guilt as I thought of him devouring crumbs pushed through bars, his purple cloaked stripped from his back, kicked and spat upon, degraded beyond all measure. Then I thought of everything he had done, how his cowardice allowed cities of the east to be taken, and how he had been willing to sacrifice Zenobia because of his own jealousy, because he was afraid of her and of Odenathus, because he wanted to punish the king of Palmyra, that she might die, or that she could survive and secure him the peace he so desperately needed at the cost of our beloved Palmyra.

Was his life, the life of the emperor, the life of a Caesar, worth the safety of the kingdom of Syria? To Zenobia it was, and to Zabbai it was, because they knew they could not have left here alive, and they knew too that if Syria fell beneath Valerian's vanity, then Rome would fall, too.

Another night slipped by. Had Zenobia reached our army? Had she managed to convince Valerian to meet with Shapur and seek terms? I prayed to the gods that she had, and had not let slip that it was a deception, and that she had not told Odenathus, for who knew what he would do in his loyalty for to Rome? I wondered too whether the trap had indeed been set, the location chosen, Valerian in unknowing agreement. Then my thoughts turned into fear. Perhaps Zenobia had not. Valerian might well have seen through the trap, discovered that Zenobia knew of his willingness to sacrifice Palmyra. And who knew if she had even made it back to our camp?

Two weeks of misery, of thirst and hunger and waiting. Two weeks since we had first entered the Persian camp, Zenobia,

Zabbai and me. The sun was low and burning morning red. I was dragged from my cage, a place that had become my own, that I had begun to think I would never leave, and my hands were tied behind me, thin twine cutting deep. My body was weak and limp and hurt. I wore only a light, filthy tunic, my armour gone.

I slumped, the guards taking my weight.

'Where are we going?' I could not sound hostile. The hard edge that I had heard before in my own voice was no longer there, now it was empty and hollow.

Persian insults were grunted back, women and children stood close by, hissing and spitting, cursing, no doubt, in their foreign tongue. But I could do nothing, arms pulled back, wrists tied, enemy warriors dragging me to the edge of the camp.

A dozen more waited. They wore armour, but carried no weapons. I was bundled onto a horse, lashed wrists tied to the pommel so that I could not fall. I grunted in pain as I swayed, the twine cutting deeper, pain coursing through every muscle and bone.

A moment later we were joined by another rider. A heavy bulk sat atop a huge horse. The whole group dipped their heads in acknowledgement of this new rider, and I realised it was Shapur himself.

He did not look at me, nor did he speak with me. He wore chainmail armour, silks strapped atop, and on his head he wore a pointed helmet. Beneath his helmet jewels glinted, his beard covering the lower half of his face. He spoke quickly with his men, talk I could not understand, and we began to move, the bright standard of the Persian army floating overhead.

Did Valerian come? I wondered. A faint hope, a warmth I had not felt for many cold nights on the desert plain, was kindled within me.

We came to a halt. Two men kicked up dust as they rode away on horseback, one to our left, and the other to our right. The others waited. I hated waiting. I always hated waiting. Knowing that you might wait a heartbeat, a mere moment, or maybe hours or days. And I hated it most then, after weeks inside a cage in the Persian camp. I could take it no more. Sat atop a horse, the pain I felt unbearable, I was aware of the long moments, of the rocky hills to one side of me stretching upward to where nomads kept flocks, and on my other side woods creeping close, shadowing the land beyond. I was aware of it all, and yet time did not seem like the passage of a moment. I was aware, and I could feel, but I did not experience the beats of my heart and the breaths I took. My mind was muddied.

Everyone dismounted. The two men returned breathless, horses foaming white at the mouth. They nodded to the Persian king and words were exchanged. And again, we waited. Consciousness faded in and out. Blurs of movement before half-open eyes slipped and slid in the sands, and the redness of morning was hard.

I forced open my eyes, to keep them open, knowing something was there, far in the distance, that it was not a blur, a figment of my imagination, the conjuring of thirst and hunger. From the hills to the east came a small company. The warriors around me prickled with tension. The group, a dozen perhaps, came nearer, closing the gap between us. Gradually coming into focus.

Ten, eleven figures riding camels and horses? I could not quite make them out. But then I saw the long hair of Zenobia, the waves reaching her waist, and the man wearing a purple cloak beside her.

They halted a few hundred paces away. With the aid of a soldier, Valerian dismounted. Zenobia jumped lithely from her camel. Zabbai, dressed full in leather armour, made a solid thud as he hit the earth. Attendants waited with the beasts as the company approached.

The emperor came with his own interpreter, though Shapur's sufficed for both men.

'I am told you are willing to discuss terms,' Valerian said.

I looked at him carefully, my eyes open now, my attention more constant. He was thinner than I remembered, gaunt, his fear hidden beneath a thin mask of pride.

Shapur's interpreter translated the Emperor's words, and Valerian gave a curt nod. Beside him, Zenobia looked at me, as though asking unsaid forgiveness, regretting having left me in the Persian camp. I could not blame her. I had told her to leave me there, knowing she would return. And now I basked in her gaze, warm and sunlit. Her brow and thin mouth were taut with anguish. I returned a weak smile in an attempt to reassure her.

Shapur spoke. The emperor's translator looked at his master with terror in his eyes and repeated: 'The King of the Sassanian Empire says he does not think your offer of the Palmyrene Kingdom will be enough.'

Valerian scowled, his eyes suddenly panicked.

'I laid out my proposition. If you did not accept, why did you agree to meet me?'

Again the words were translated into Persian, and Shapur smiled.

'There has been another offer put to me. Far more tempting. Far greater than yours. One that I have decided to accept.'

Valerian opened his mouth, as if to speak, panic now laced with confusion. But a sound like thunder shook the ground, rolling across the hills, and the horses and camels stood there in the middle of the desert whinnied and paced.

A torrent of men on horses headed toward us. Hundreds of them. No screams or cries of battle rage. No banging of drums. Just the thudding of hooves and the faint chink of metal.

All sound ceased as we were encircled. Our fate, the fate of the emperor, now hung with Shapur. I realised my breath came quickly. But Zenobia was as calm as if she sat in the gardens of her father's villa. She must have known this would happen, and yet I felt fear, not knowing if even now we would not leave alive.

'Who are these men?' Valerian demanded. Then, with a shaking voice, 'What is this? We agreed, twelve men, nothing more.'

Shapur, with his hefty frame and unmerciful posture, stepped closer to the emperor.

'You are Caesar Publius Licinius Valerianus Augustus? Emperor of the Roman Empire?' He waited as his words were repeated in Latin.

Valerian, his face hollow and pale, nodded confirmation.

'Palmyra would never have been enough. You caused much amusement amongst my people the day you sent a woman to plead her own city of marble for your own peace. You think to resist me, to repel my invasion, and when you realise you cannot, you think to throw scraps as if to your dogs in the hope that I might take them? You think that of us, Emperor of Rome? And yet you forget, I am no leader of warriors, no desert tribe. I have my own empire. I am a king of Persia, of the House Sasan. I am the King of Kings and I do not bow to your empire. I will give the people of Syria peace, but the price of that peace is your life. You are *my* prisoner.'

Valerian choked. 'I am no one's prisoner!' Incensed, he spat at Zenobia, 'Odenathus betrayed me.' He started forward, his features contorted with loathing. 'I am emperor of Rome, and he a client king. A man whom we had the good grace to allow to rule in these lands.'

He made to grab her, but she stepped back and looked him square in the face.

'No. We were your people, your subjects. Odenathus was more loyal to you and to the Roman Empire than any man I have known. You found a good man in him, a trusted man. But you lost our faith with ill-judged decisions, with incompetence and pettiness. You would have given Palmyra to Shapur to save face, sacrificed those who are loyal to you. Even I know of Shapur's generosity to his own, to those who would follow him, to the kings beneath him. He would not have stooped so low as to do what you have done to us. Even your own men, those loyal to Rome, have begun to turn against you. How do you think they,' she jerked her head to the hundreds of warriors surrounding us, 'went unnoticed by your own scouts; your own Praetorian Guard?'

I looked beyond Zenobia. Ballista, the Praetorian Prefect, the man whom I had seen in Valerian's house as we spoke of seeking peace with Shapur. Only now he wore his armour and not an off-white toga. His helmet and red plume stood high on his head. And his eyes, shaded beneath the rim, were cold and hard and focussed on no one.

Valerian looked as if he had been struck. Two guards from the Persian company stepped forward, swords drawn. Valerian looked about him, one last glance at the small group that had once been his people.

'Ballista!' he shouted, but the man did not move. No one in the Roman company moved. Not one appeared willing to save their emperor's life, and I realised suddenly how easily the empowered fall, how hard their landing must be. The greatest man in Rome betrayed by his own people. And for a moment I consoled myself with the knowledge of what he had done to his Christian people, for their belief, and for what he would have done to Palmyra.

Persian soldiers wrestled Valerian to his hands and knees. One brought a horse up beside him. Another soldier kicked his head until his face was down-turned and I knew I flinched, my own face throbbing in unison, just as Zabbai did. Zenobia, however, looked at him without emotion.

Shapur walked up to Valerian and placed a heavy booted foot upon the emperor's back. Valerian tried to get up, to stand, but received another kick and I heard the break of his nose, perhaps of his teeth and jaw.

Shapur's full weight forced Valerian's back to curve further. Blood dripped from his mouth and nose, spattering the white sand as the King of Persia, the King of Kings, the son of Ardashir and founder of the Sassanian Empire, used Valerian, Emperor of Rome, as a stepping-stone to mount his horse.

I could have cried for the shame I felt then, that we, the

Syrians, the Palmyrenes, had done this to a man who had been our own, to the emperor so respected by Odenathus; that we could have done it to any man. A man now defeated and broken and betrayed.

He allowed himself to be dragged to his feet and led away by the Persians. In one, sweeping moment he had lost everything: imperium, title, status, troops, family and country. He had lost his entire empire, and he had lost his pride. Everything had gone.

Shapur turned his beast and said to Zenobia, 'You are a capable woman, Palmyrene Queen. You kept your promise.'

'Will you keep yours?' she asked, voice cold and without fear.

'Our forces will begin to move in the next few days,' he said dismissively. He went to turn away then seemed to check himself. He looked at her long and hard. His horse tossed its head from side to side in agitation.

'If you had been another person, on another occasion, I would have killed you for the disloyalty you have shown your emperor. I cannot bargain with a woman or a man who would turn traitor as you have done. But I am unsure about you, Palmyrene Queen. You are different.

'I do not let you or your friends leave here alive because of my word, or because you are a woman. No, I will let you leave because you are a true warrior. You knew the dangers awaiting you in my camp; I can see in your eyes the unknown and uncertainty, and yet you came anyway. You face what you are afraid of, and you know the consequences. You left behind the one you love, not knowing if he would live. And you did what you have done not for yourself but for your people, and so I cannot call you traitor, even though you are. If you were a man, you would be a warrior. Maybe I will call you warrior,' he said, then paused so his words could be translated. 'That will fit you well.' He nodded, satisfied with himself. 'To my people, you will be known as *The Warrior Queen*.'

Shapur waved me across to where Zenobia, Zabbai and the Roman soldiers stood. I almost wept with relief and with pain.

Shapur laughed; the most animated I had known him. Zenobia half-smiled and I knew then that in this Persian king she had found something of an equal.

Shapur waved a hand overhead and the mass of Persian warriors began to disperse and we were left alone on the plain.

The wind plucked at my hair and my body was so tired I would not have stayed mounted but for the cord cutting into my wrists tying me to the horse. Zabbai crossed to me, cut my bonds and climbed on the horse behind me to help keep me upright.

'We head back to our own camp now,' he said. 'Fear not, Zabdas, we will see you right.'

Zenobia averted her gaze.

'There is much to be done,' Ballista said, removing his helmet. 'Not all of my men knew of what you intended and the news must be managed with care.'

Zenobia nodded and Ballista replaced his helmet.

They set off, and as Zabbai held the reins of my horse, guiding us back to our own people, I watched Shapur riding across the sands. He followed his men as they dragged Valerian behind them, heading for the Persian camp to decide the fate of an emperor, and I smelt my own freedom on the heavy, grey air.

CHAPTER II

Samira – 290 AD (Present day)

I AM LEANING OVER the side of the boat, peering down at murky water and I glance up and I see my grandfather run fingers through white streaked hair beneath the heat of the sun. I squint at him, but he does not look at me, does not see the scorn still upon my face and my confusion.

He had played a part in treachery. He and Zenobia, and I find I cannot forgive them that, for sending a man to an inevitable fate, no matter what he has done. I am unable to make sense, to turn the tables and see events from their perspective, to look upon their actions as if I were there and knew what it was to be at war with Valerian Caesar leading men and doing it so badly.

And I am angry with myself for not understanding and with my grandfather because I cannot agree, I cannot change my feelings and thoughts and know his and Zenobia's decisions would have been my own, and yet I want them to be so very much.

I am struggling to believe, unable to comprehend betrayal, this betrayal of a man that should have been respected and admired. Yet I know he could not be, because he was no emperor like Gallienus was emperor, he could not hold respect or authority. And so what then? What to do? Can what they did be determined as right?

'Did Zenobia not feel guilt for what she did?' I ask him.

The water rushes beneath my gaze, green and blue and white,

and I am mesmerized by the movement and by my thoughts.

'She did not,' he says. 'Zenobia only felt guilt for leaving me in the Persian camp. She had no guarantee that I would leave there alive, with or without the deliverance of the emperor.'

'But how could she not feel guilt, for subjecting an emperor to a life of imprisonment and for turning against the Empire of Rome and for all of that?'

'Because she could not,' he says simply. 'The moment her father secured her a seat on the Palmyrene council, she had a duty to protect and to serve the people of that city, a duty which became a far greater responsibility when she married Odenathus and became queen. She saw her people, those of Syria, suffer, and the only way to make it stop was to stop Valerian. So the answer is no, she felt no guilt, because she could not allow herself to.'

I am struggling again, because I know he is right, that Zenobia could not allow herself to feel too much, to have her will bent by the fate of others. I understand that and the effort it must have taken …

Silence falls between us and it is still and heavy in the air and I feel suddenly tired.

I am young and my eyes are keen and I see the people roaming the roads on land as we drift out of the valley, children playing on the shore and the happiness in them. The air here is pungent and I smell rotting wood mingled with rich spices on the breeze.

'Shapur called her a warrior queen,' I say. 'I have heard the same myself.'

'You will have done. She was known as such by many.'

'Was she?' I ask, thinking of a queen in armour and with sword and shield clutched in thin and delicate fingers. I think of myself in her place, and I feel only the weight of responsibility and I am more tired still.

'Zenobia was a warrior queen in more ways than one. Shapur's words were the first I heard which truly described the difference between a soldier and a warrior. A warrior is someone who knows the danger and faces it, head on, regardless. Zenobia

Zabdas - 290 AD (Present day)

was certainly that. She defied not only Rome, but also her king and her husband. To her, it never mattered what others thought. She was content to do what *she* thought was right.'

I am thinking and I feel suddenly the knot in my stomach, the fate which awaited her. Rome might never know she betrayed their emperor, just as I have never known and many others would not, but there is one who would and I am already afraid of the king's discovery and what he would do.

'What did Odenathus do when you returned without the emperor? He cannot have known that Zenobia was intending to betray Valerian?'

'I have told you enough for today,' he says.

'You cannot leave the tale there!' I say, annoyed and frustrated and eager to know more.

'Not now, Samira,' he says, and I know he is tired also.

His eyes hang heavy and he is not concentrating. He is gaining in years, I know, and I am afraid of the day when he will leave me as my father has, but I hope it is a long time from now, and of old age and failing health, and not to the edge of an enemy sword. Yet I know that is not what he would want. He would die in battle and he would break the heart of me, his granddaughter, and Bamdad would too, and as grandfather turns and retires to his cabin there are tears in my eyes.

They are the tears of someone who is tired and who has known too much these past weeks. It is catching me, the late nights with my grandfather's men and the slaves we have set free and my father's passing, and it is all too much in this moment.

I am thinking of him. I cannot help myself. Vaballathus, my father, the rogue I have loved and who has loved me in return, who cared for me. And yet he could not help himself, he could not stay from enemy swords and out of danger.

I have grieved and yet now, with a yawn and thoughts only for my bed, he is creeping into my mind and he is bringing with him great sadness. I am alone. I have my grandfather and I have Bamdad, but both are gaining in years and neither are my age;

neither a childhood friend. And neither of them can be here with warm arms around me. They are not as Aurelia was to my grandfather, always there, always waiting for him, a caring and loving soul that would be beside him through each night no matter what he had done nor who he had killed.

They give me everything they can but they cannot give me this. Whatever that might be.

'It is late.'

I cannot take my eyes from the water for I cannot look up at the person who speaks. I do not wish them to see my red-rimmed eyes and to know I have been crying for the father I cannot have returned to me and the loneliness I feel.

He places an arm on my curved back and I feel the stroke of his fingers against my coarse tunic. It is as if he has read my mind; knows my thoughts and come to me, but I do not believe that. I know men cannot read minds. They read only what they see.

I turn into him, without looking at him.

My face is against his chest and his arms are around me and my tears will not stop, they will not cease, but they are silent.

'This is not a good place for a young woman,' he says.

I can smell him, the spike of leather and oak and salt.

I say nothing. I do not pull away. I do not dare to look up at him and for him to see my face. I am wishing this man who holds me, who grips me firmly, was another man, a man my age, a man who has begun to create a warmth in me that I do not fully understand, but I know that I want to feel it again, to have his arms about me, and know that I have begun to forgive the things I never thought I would.

'Ah, *Rubetta*, come now, there's no need for tears.'

Bamdad takes my shoulders in his hands and stoops down to look me directly in the eye. He grins a broad grin, one designed to force me to smile back at him.

'It's late,' he says, 'and you're tired. A good night's sleep is all you need.'

Zabdas - 290 AD (Present day)

I nod. I know he is right. I know that I can no longer stifle a yawn and that I have stopped crying but my eyes are so very heavy and wishing for slumber.

CHAPTER 12

Zabdas – 260 AD

I WAS HUNGRY AND I was thirsty, my mouth drier than the sands upon which we rode, and I felt utter exhaustion as we approached the city of Edessa, where the remaining Roman and Syrian legions lay. Ballista had ridden hard ahead to speak with the Praetorian Guard. Zabbai had breathed no words after we had parted with Shapur; his mind, I think, plagued by what had happened, the treachery we were all party to. And yet Zenobia appeared only to concern herself with matters of what would happen next.

As our small company came within the shadow of Edessa's walls, I saw a figure running from the main gate, crying my name, her feet kicking plumes of dust from the roadway. Soldiers attempted to block her passage but she pushed them aside.

Aurelia.

I slid down from my horse and she ran into my arms and she cried upon my shoulder.

'I am returned,' I said, brushing her hair with my hand. 'I have come back.'

Once inside the city, Zenobia sought Odenathus.

'He will be angry with you, Zenobia,' Zabbai said.

'You did not tell him what you intended to do?' I know I

sounded shocked, but I should not have been, for the knowledge did not surprise me.

'He knows of the meet and that we accompanied Valerian Caesar, but he knows nothing of what we have done,' she replied.

'And what of me?' I asked. Odenathus must have known of my absence, wondered where I was, suspected my being held by the Persians.

Zabbai said: 'I led Odenathus to believe that Shapur detained you as assurance against Valerian failing to attend the meet; that Shapur wanted a Syrian messenger to send back with his displeasure.'

As he spoke, I could not help but think of my flesh stripped from living skin and I shuddered. The peeling and the pain; the blood and the muscle.

We found Odenathus waiting in the house Emperor Valerian had once commandeered. Even after such a short time, it already seemed subdued and lifeless, the walls and floors grey, the lamps unlit, as if knowing the last occupant would never return.

The king met us in the hallway, his large, sturdy figure striding towards us. His look one of anxiety.

'You are returned,' he said, and put a hand affectionately upon Zenobia's shoulder. 'And you also, Zabdas! I am grateful for that. The Roman generals have been waiting but have now left—' He gestured behind him to another room, then stared at us, his last words hanging.

'What happened? Where is Valerian?'

'The Emperor Valerian has been taken captive.' Zenobia's words contained no emotion, nor any pause. She delivered the news as swiftly as one would lift a cup of water to parched lips.

'And yet you are here?' Odenathus' face became laced with confusion and fury. He looked between us but none spoke. Finally he breathed, 'What have you done?'

'Valerian has been taken captive by Shapur. The meet was never to discuss peace, but to fulfil a bargain made between myself and the Persians. Syria is now free of the one man stopping us from pressing Shapur back into Persia,' Zenobia replied, her expression impassive.

'You have done what?' Odenathus' voice was little more than a whisper of disbelief.

'Using Zabdas as security, I bargained with the Shapur that if I gave them the Emperor of Rome, they would leave Syria in peace.'

For long moments the king seemed incapable of speech. He set his mouth in a firm line, and closed his eyes briefly. When he opened them he said: 'You have betrayed the Empire and everything I believe in. This was not your choice. It was never a decision you should have made, nor were you entitled to make it. You have made fools of us and you have made an enemy of Rome. Have you any notion of what they will do when they discover your actions?'

'They will discover nothing,' she replied coldly.

'What in the name of all the gods do you mean, Zenobia? How can you possibly keep this from them? You have just bargained with the life of the Emperor of the Roman Empire, the most powerful man in the world! For the love of Bel there is no turning back from this!'

'Valerian's Praetorian prefect, Ballista, knew of what we planned. He rides now to inform those who did not know, but if we are accountable to Rome, then so are the Romans themselves. They have turned on their own emperor, and they will be at this very moment jostling for power in the east. Those who resist Ballista will be put to the sword.'

'Ballista? Gods, I had thought that man to be Valerian's most trusted man, his advisor!'

Zenobia shook her head, her face hard.

'You know as well as any of us that Valerian's own men have been dissatisfied. It was obvious. They talked amongst themselves, and they talked to their women. That is how I discovered their willingness to assist me. If I had not given Valerian over to the Persians and hidden the usurpation of Ballista, then he would have killed Valerian anyway. We would have been subject to internal war and discontent—those who believed in the Emperor standing against those who did not. Instead the Romans will think their Emperor fallen to the Persians rather than betrayed. Instead we will suffer a jostle for power, but you have a right to that to. You are as much a Roman as any I have met in Rome. You have a claim to the purple just as Ballista does.'

'What do you expect to happen now, Zenobia? You think my taking the purple will see you the peace you want? Gods, you are your father's daughter! You cannot have peace when you are at war!'

'We are always at war with one frontier or another.'

'And yet now we are at war with both.'

'You have been at war with yourself for many years, husband. I do this for you and for Syria. We would have fallen beneath the might of Shapur. The armies of Rome are yours if you would simply take them. And then we can march on the Persians.'

'Shapur told you this? And you believed him? You have agreed peace with them. You would go back on your word?' Odenathus spat.

'Shapur will never give us peace. The terms were a ruse. We both knew that they would not be upheld. I knew as I gave Shapur the emperor that we would not see a peace after that one act. Shapur has no morals with his enemies, no desire to uphold what he promises. And yet I believe he thinks we do. He will expect us to retreat now in the wake of the peace negotiated.'

'And you!' Odenathus turned on Zabbai. 'You knew of this?' I heard anger in his tone, but I also sensed hurt, a betrayal that the king did not understand.

'Not at first. I had no knowledge of the plan until we reached the Persian camp on our first visit. But in reality, Zenobia had little choice—'

'Silence,' Odenathus said, his voice low but forceful. 'I do not want to hear your reasoning. Your actions are inexcusable and you should have known better than this; you of all people,

Zabbai. Rome will never forgive us. And they would never accept my rule. Who would support me in that, Zenobia? We have turned against the Empire, against the still ruling emperor, Gallienus. They will seek a revenge on us like none other for what you have done.'

'They will not,' Zenobia said. 'They have no reason to suspect what has passed. And if Rome suspects anyone, it will be Ballista and not you. He was Valerian's Praetorian prefect, he was there as we handed the emperor over to the Persians.'

Odenathus' anger subsided, his shoulders dropped, his face drained of feeling. He did not answer, he just shook his head. Some small fragment of him knew what Zenobia had done was in the best interests of Syria, I was sure. He must have seen that she had no choice. Or would he rather she had given up her life in doing Rome's bidding, had her body returned to him flayed, and to know that it was caused by his own loyalty to an empire which cared so little in return. And yet I could sense from the look on his face that she had gone too far, she had betrayed everything he believed in; the one thing he had sworn loyalty to. She had betrayed his empire and its emperor; his superior, his overlord.

He rubbed his forehead with both hands.

'You need to call a council of all the generals, my lord,' Zabbai urged.

'What?' Odenathus said, lost in the weight of what had been done. Nothing could change it now.

'My king,' Zenobia pressed.

'Do not call me that,' he hissed. 'You wilfully disobey me; how can I possibly be your king. Where is the respect you owe me, as your husband and your master? Where is your loyalty? Where is your pride?'

He turned away.

'Odenathus,' Zabbai beckoned, 'you need to move quickly if you want to secure the Roman army and your position. Please, what has been done cannot be undone. The east needs you, just as it always has. We sit on a knife edge; Rome on one side, the Persians on the other. Only you can command the obedience of the army and defeat our enemies. Please, my friend, do not waste this opportunity.'

Finally, Odenathus appeared to stir from his solitary thoughts and nodded. Without looking at Zenobia, he ordered Zabbai to send for the Stratego of the Palmyrene army and those of the Roman army to join him in the house.

'We must do our best to turn this situation to our advantage,' Odenathus said, and though it was a slight on Zenobia's actions, she did not flinch or show any reaction to his words. Taking little notice of me, he turned to face her. 'Zabbai will be back with the Stratego within the hour. You are not needed here.'

'You may not approve of what I have done, but I am still a member of the Palmyrene council. I have every right to stay and be a part of what happens now.'

'Will your ambition never cease, Zenobia? Have you not done enough?' Odenathus looked disappointed, his eyes were at once sorrow and anger. 'I have only ever asked that you be my wife and bear my children. You have failed in both.' His voice rose with the honesty of his words, and the truth of them checked me. On both counts she had failed, though the latter through no fault of her own. Or did some of the blame for her lost child lie with her own actions? Did Odenathus blame her for always wanting to be present, for being in Antioch with him instead of behind the safe walls of Palmyra? Did he think she had walked too far as the citizens of Antioch fled as the city fell? I had thought so at that time, but whether it caused her to lose her child, no one could know.

In those moments, I doubt Odenathus saw it as such. He saw a woman who had become his wife and a queen turn against him, ignore his will, defy his authority, betray the empire that had made him king and lose their unborn child. Grief, confusion and despair seemed to overcome him. I could see the waves of emotion in his eyes, spilling into the contours of his face.

'You have failed me in every conceivable way.'

Perhaps he thought to humble her, to break her strength and for her to know his authority, but her face only hardened with each accusation. Deep within, I suspected she would be hurting, her surety crumbling and emotion bubbling inside. But on the outside she looked at her lord, master and husband with contempt.

'If you wish to rule then do so. We brought armies back from Rome, and now I give them solely to you. But you must grasp them now, not later. Do as you have sworn to do for your country and protect her.'

Zenobia's final words punched the air with force. Odenathus recoiled and even I, at whom the words were not aimed, felt shaken by them. For a heartbeat she watched the king, to see perhaps the effect of her words, and then she walked away and the whole place took on an eerie, chill silence.

After a moment, I made to follow her.

'Wait,' Odenathus said.

I turned back, expecting his wrath for my part in the plan to turn Valerian over to the Persians. He had every right to feel anger at me, for my agreement to stay behind to secure the bargain, even though it could scarcely be called a choice.

'My lord?'

'Why does she insist upon disobeying me?' he asked. Although I was the only person present, I did not feel the question was directed at me. 'Have I not given her everything she could possibly want? Have I not bestowed upon her the power she requested, that her father wanted? Her father dreamed of a palace like those of Egypt, in which his wife could live out her days in the luxury from which she came. Julius has beliefs, but all told he is a man who enjoys the simplicities in life. When Zenobia became my wife, I gave his family everything they desired. Everything they could possibly want.'

Odenathus slumped into a chair, his whole body ebbing of energy. I felt sorry for him then for the first time. There was something missing between him and Zenobia, a connection lacking. They were both strong-willed, they both had and desired a certain power, and yet their opinions differed. Not by much, for they both wanted peace, they both desired a safe Syria, but by was enough to cause great rifts.

'Emperor Valerian offered Palmyra in exchange for peace,' I replied.

Odenathus opened his mouth to speak but checked himself. He stared at me, as if I had said something absurd, a foreign phrase he could no more understand than I had understood Shapur's Persian words.

'Palmyra? He tried to exchange Palmyra? Valerian never mentioned this to me. He would have given *my* city to the Persians in exchange for what? He could not have had peace in exchange for Palmyra; Shapur would never have agreed to that. How could he be so blind?'

'Shapur told us as much. He said he would never have agreed to the bargain put to him by Valerian. It is why Zenobia offered something else … something more,' I said carefully. Lies, I thought, but I did not care, it might well smooth the tension between them.

Odenathus did not reply, and so I, too, sat with caution upon one of the luxurious chairs, which only served to remind my limbs of how much I needed to eat, drink and sleep in the comfort of my own bed, Aurelia's thin, warm, innocently pale arms around me. I began to drift with those thoughts, until the king spoke again.

'You know Zenobia well, Zabdas. Better, I think, than I know her myself.'

'I do not think so. I think I barely know her much of the time. I did not predict any of this …'

'It is merely an observation, Zabdas,' he said, and I realised he mistook my words as a defence, that he might be offended if I knew her better than her own husband.

He groaned, low and long, leaning back in his chair and

allowing everything to wash over him.

'Sometimes, I do not think she understands, just like her father does not understand. We have been under Rome's protection for so long. In the past they may not have given us the support we needed to vanquish the enemy, but they stationed legions here; they gave us enough to hold the enemy at bay. Who knows what will happen now? They could turn against us. We know not whether Ballista or any one of Valerian's generals will attempt to usurp Gallienus. Many will think I betrayed Rome, and those close will know that Zenobia did. There will be a new jostle for power, and all the while we will succumb to invaders. What Zenobia has done … I cannot see how it will help us.'

I was unsure whether I was required to answer so I said: 'Julius thinks severing ourselves from Rome is the only way to survive, Lord King. He thinks that the Empire is coming to an end, crumbling beneath the weight of its own corruption, and that to stand a chance of survival we must reinforce ourselves and not rely upon the Romans. He worries that they will pull their legions out of Syria, and we will be left to the Persians' mercy.'

'They might well do that now, Zabdas. And Julius does believe that, indeed.' The king nodded. 'Julius has been a friend to me for a long time. We were friends as children. We grew up together, trained together, fought in the army together for years. We travelled to Egypt; spent our youth fighting and drinking. And yet still we disagree.'

'I knew you were friends, and that you had known one another a long time, but I did not know it was quite that long.'

Odenathus raised his eyebrows. 'No? There was a time when we were inseparable. Skinning our knees and fighting with wooden swords—and that was when we were still in our cribs! But there were expectations of me, and not of Julius. My father had been king for a long time before me, and he taught me the way to survive, to rule long and to know the respect of my people, and that can only be done by keeping them safe, by ensuring they are well-fed, that trade is profitable. Give them a good life and they will respect you for what you have done for them. Julius could believe what he wanted, to think how he liked. I envied him that.' He laughed, but the laughter was followed by an awkward silence.

'You think I kept you from combat, sent you to Rome, because you were incapable?' he went on. 'Not so. You know already it was because Julius wished for me to keep you from harm.' Suddenly he looked tired again. 'When he agreed to defend our frontier against the Tanukh, he asked for more than just Zenobia's position on the council, something I have long regretted. He asked that I protect you both against all harm. I was not to allow you to follow him south, as you so adamantly wished. You were to stay safe. Rome, I viewed, was safer than here, so I sent you both, but I have been forced to break many promises, including those to Julius. Emperor Valerian forced me to break my word when he demanded you and Zenobia seek to meet with King Shapur, and Zenobia compounded it when she secured her bargain with your life.'

He sighed heavily.

'So, you see, I have participated in your well-being more than you think, and I can only ask your forgiveness that I have so far been unsuccessful in keeping you from harm. How I will explain to Julius the danger in which I have placed you both, I do not know. He told me to protect you.'

As he finished, anger rolled over me. My mouth ran with saliva and I could no longer focus. The revelation of what had been agreed between the man I loved as a father and the man I had learned to hate was more than I could comprehend. That Odenathus truly sought our safety, and had failed to such an extent, sickened me.

'But you did not.'

'No, I did not.'

He looked awkward again, then seemed to summon the will to continue.

'Julius' inability to have a son is something I have never really understood. My own son has been nothing but a disappointment to me, failing to obey orders, to seek the advice of those with much greater experience than himself, making simple errors that have seen the deaths of so many. I am charged with protecting my people, and I failed them because he failed me. Why would Julius want a son who would let him down? His daughter has become a queen and his family have wealth and security. More now than ever before. But I did understand. When Julius told me of you, that he had found the son of Meskenit, I saw it then. I heard it in his voice; the excitement, the longing, the completeness. He cares for you as if you were his own.'

'I barely know him,' I confessed.

Odenathus smiled, though it was more of a grimace. 'He told me that you are the boy he never had, that he feels more complete now he has found you. He searched for you for such a long time. I dare say another man would not have been so determined.'

I wanted to ask the king more. I wanted to discover everything I could of Julius, but I did not have chance as heavy footsteps sounded in the corridor and a moment later Zabbai returned.

Odenathus gave me a curt nod indicating the end of our conversation, and stood.

'The Roman generals and our Stratego await you,' Zabbai said.

'Ask them to come through,' Odenathus replied.

The commanding men entered the room. Amongst them were Ballista, hard-faced and without any appearance of shame for what he had conspired with Zenobia. And I saw Pouja, with whom I had fought at the gates of Antioch.

'Gentlemen, for those of you who have not already heard,' he said, motioning to Ballista, 'it is for me to deliver the outcome of Emperor Valerian's meet with Shapur.'

He scanned the others before him, Roman generals and commanders in the Syrian armies alike, holding each gaze for a brief moment.

'There is no treaty. The enemy have taken Valerian Caesar captive.'

Uproar followed as each man shouted in protest, declaring the act one of unforgivable evil, and demanding something be done. Only a few of the Praetorian Guard remained silent.

'Quiet,' Odenathus bellowed. 'Please. We cannot dwell on what has passed. We must look forward.'

'How did this happen?' a Roman demanded. 'The meet was by mutual agreement.'

'Shapur went back on his word,' Odenathus replied, 'and Valerian walked into a trap.'

'The Persian bastards! We must make a stand. We need to secure the frontier. This is one loss too many. Rome does not allow its enemies to gain the advantage. Never!' another Roman general said loudly, seconded by another.

Odenathus had surprised me with his sudden change in front of the generals. It was what made him a king, I reflected, to stand in front of your men and lead them with confidence you may not feel and words you may not mean, and in your heart you are afraid of what may come.

'Agreed,' Odenathus said. 'We must show them we will move no further. Too long have the Persians threatened the Empire, ravaged the eastern lands. Enough,' he said, slamming the fist of one hand into the palm of his other.

'Who will lead the Roman legions?' Pouja said.

'Odenathus could take command if he is willing,' the first Roman general said, and I noted that Ballista was not surprised by his colleague's words. 'We would be willing to fight beneath your command until Gallienus gives other orders. We must send word to him. Tell him what has happened to his father. He will come himself, I think.'

'No,' Ballista said from back of the room. He still wore his armour, his crested helmet beneath his arm. There was no mistaking his rank, nor his desire to maintain control over the Romans. 'If Valerian has been taken, my men will answer to me, and I answer only to Gallienus. With all due respect, Odenathus, we might have failed to gain advantage beneath Valerian Caesar, but there is nothing to say your leadership will see us a better position. Your kingship is disputable at best, ruling a client kingdom only. Any one of us,' he gestured to the Roman generals, 'seconded by the men, is in a position to take control.' The deep lines of Ballista's face creased and he looked long and hard at Odenathus, as if willing him to counter.

'And each and every one of us has sworn allegiance to Rome.' Odenathus said. 'I have no quarrel with you, but this is my country and I know these lands, our enemy, and my own men. I would see command of my forces, and you are welcome to take command of your own. We can lead the combined armies of Syria and Rome into battle against the Persians together. We both know we must push the Persians back, and we all know that Shapur will come at us with greater force than ever before, believing us weakened after the fall of Valerian.'

All the Roman commanders looked to the Praetorian prefect, waiting for him to speak again. Eventually he spat, 'You had better lead well, King Odenathus; as well as I, if we are to work with one another. I have respect for what you have accomplished in the past, but our numbers are small, even with our armies combined. We are less than the Persians. The plague appears to have ceased spreading, but our legions are depleted.'

It seemed ironic that the man should speak of weak leaders, when Odenathus could be no worse than Valerian in his cowardice and his attempted betrayal of Palmyra.

More arguments ensued, until finally Pouja demanded, 'Then we are agreed?'

Perhaps they were, or perhaps it was Pouja's motion and stance that caused the murmur of agreement that followed. They could have argued all night, I was sure, but we did not have time.

As they left, Odenathus gave me a look of sympathetic exhaustion, and I thought perhaps he was sorry then for what I had endured in the Persian camp, that perhaps we were both close to Zenobia but neither of us truly knew her. I shared his look with a grimace.

'You are dismissed, Zabdas. Go and find your woman. Rest, while you can.'

'Gratitude, my Lord.'

I stumbled outside, into the early evening air. It was cool and fresh and pleasant on my skin. I looked about me for Zabbai, to bid him a few words of thanks for his part in returning to the Persian army for me, and for simply being there and for mounting my horse behind me and seeing me safely back. He was a general, and whether or not it was the exhaustion playing a merry tune inside me, we had crossed so much land together and I thought of him as friend in those moments.

There was no sight of him, but neither could I see Pouja and the other Syrian Stratego. I was alone.

The streets were still, the slow murmur of the people of Edessa in adjacent streets. I set off, back to Aurelia, back to warmth, back to something that was not fear and a stinking cage. My mind began to shut down on the thoughts whirring within. In one day, the Emperor of Rome had been taken captive by the enemy, I was set free, Odenathus had taken back his legions in Syria, and Zenobia had become a traitor to Rome.

CHAPTER 13

Zabdas – 260 AD

EXHAUSTED, I LET THE thought of my bed take over me, but I had not walked far when I heard raised voices. Arguing. Not wanting to disturb, unsure of who I might see or the nature of their disagreement, I slipped out of sight.

'Valerian was always concerned about the power he held. You know that as well as the rest of us.'

'He was, that is true, I cannot deny it, but we both know he is a great general, that he will lead his own armies well.'

There was a pause. I heard footfalls. Then shadows passed by.

'Odenathus' control is growing; more so now. I heard that Ballista will lead the Romans, but even then, who is to say he will keep power over the legions?'

There was a grunt of agreement. 'Then we need to eliminate the problem. Odenathus cannot stand in our way.'

'We can do nothing before we have the authority.'

'Then we need to …' but their voices trailed off into the darkness.

My heart raced, pounding in my chest as if it would break through my ribs. I did not see their faces, but from their attire, they were Roman. I had no doubt in my mind that they plotted to see Odenathus fall from power. The game has begun, I thought. The throne of the eastern emperor is vacant.

From the moment Ballista nodded agreement to the King of

Palmyra taking command over his own legions, Odenathus once more held a good deal of power in the east. Despite the threats I heard murmured between the two Roman soldiers, the armies of Rome and those of Syria worked together. They carried out their orders; to defend the eastern frontier against the Persians. I did not tell Odenathus what I heard, but I found Zabbai in a tavern and warned him of the threat to the king's life.

'Aye, I suspected Odenathus would face opposition. There will be friction in the Roman ranks and they see Odenathus as opposition to any man attempting to take the purple,' he replied as we sat eating. 'Besides, they will worry Syria will openly rebel against Rome, and they have enough problems as it is.'

'What if they do not take orders from Gallienus?' I said. 'You think they would wait?'

The muscles beneath Zabbai's eyes tightened so that the heavy bags beneath creased. 'They might, they might not. Odenathus is a king, he has long needed to protect his own power. That will never change.

'Do you think Ballista will try to take Odenathus' command as Valerian did, and control both the Roman and the Syrian armies?'

Zabbai gave a short sniff and pushed his empty bowl away.

'I would not put it past the man. He knew of Zenobia's plan to rid us of Valerian. There have long been two Praetorian prefects because the emperors of Rome were always unwilling to put their trust in one man alone. Not that it did Valerian much good. Zenobia discovered Ballista was, like most of the Roman army, unhappy with Valerian's leadership. He arranged the scouts ahead of Valerian and us.'

I let my spoon clatter in my empty bowl and swallowed.

'And the other Praetorian Guard?'

Zabbai shrugged. 'It appears Ballista has more control over the Guard than his colleague. And Zenobia appears to enjoy playing dangerous games.'

It was as if life had breathed itself back into Odenathus. His once grim expression became lighter, the lines on his older face smoother. He commanded with skill and energy and I knew what it was to be under the command of a man who could lead. The legions were more organised, the men were trained hard and supplies were shipped in from the south to feed the thousands of hungry mouths. Meanwhile, the Romans prospered under the rule of Ballista. Both men it appeared had a skill for leadership.

The respect for the commanders grew, and so did mine.

Zenobia remained by Odenathus' side, but with greater tension between them than ever before. She had lost his trust, and even the gain in command over the eastern legions could not replenish what they once had. Cold, hurt, untrusting glances flitted between them, even though Zabbai spoke with Odenathus of her courage in an effort to reconcile them. We all tried, for we could all sense that they would make an extraordinary team in the days of freedom following the downfall of Valerian.

Instead of allowing the situation to push her into subdued silence, Zenobia would march with us all day until her feet were blistered and swollen, just as she had walked from Antioch as it fell at our backs. Only this time she walked toward the Persians, not away from them. She began to train with me and the men; wielding a light sword and throwing spears in an effort to match our skill. She would curse when she failed, and persisted, determined, sure that she could do whatever we could, insisting that she must know how to be everything and to do it all.

And at night she would drink with us.

'Another!' Zenobia said to the table at large.

She grabbed the jug and filled the cups around the table, sloshing wine on the wooden top as she did so.

I was drunk enough to need to focus carefully in order to count coins into the centre of the table and reach for the dice. I realised that in the morning I would not remember that which I was concentrating so hard on now.

The soldiers around the table were common Roman

legionaries. We trained all day in the heat, sweating, cursing, jesting and competing, and now it was time to enjoy ourselves.

Bamdad sat beside me and roared in support as I won the throw.

'Here,' Zenobia said, and thrust my cup at me. 'You need to drink more, Zabdas. Our companions may not be winning at dice, but they are certainly ahead of you in other respects.'

Soldiers thumped their fists on the wooden table-top in agreement. Zenobia dazzled them with a smile and tipped her head in acceptance of their appreciation. She had discarded her jewels and her hair was no longer braded and without oils, but hung loose and tangled and damp with the efforts of training.

She reached across the table and collected the scattered dice. She shook them overhead and let them cascade onto the table once more.

'It would seem I am lucky!'

Bamdad leaned in toward me, his breath on my cheek, and said, 'If Odenathus saw this, he would not be pleased. She flirts with the men and for what? To make him jealous? It will not work, I can tell you that.'

'Odenathus does not seem to care,' I said in a hushed voice. 'And I do not think this is to make him jealous.' I looked at the faces of the men and they were enraptured. They loved her, as the men aboard the ship back from Rome had loved her. She drew their attention. She did not sit above them, but as one of them. And in turn many soldiers accepted her company without question or hostility or reluctance.

And yet in my more sober moments I had heard other words, the murmurs in court from Odenathus' advisors. Some said she drowned herself in a mixture of sorrow and rejection, attempting to disguise her sadness and broken relations with the king. But I knew it was not that. Zenobia was much too clever and much more composed than to let herself be overcome. Each day she trained with us, and each night she drank and laughed with us. She was gaining in trust and respect day by day. She was a friend to the men, but as a queen and a woman, she earned a very delicate, generally unobtainable, presence amongst us. A few looked at her with dislike, thinking she tricked our king, worked some unseen magic upon him. More still suspected her betrayal of Emperor Valerian, and I began to hear whispers the Gods had sent her, and they began to see her as a woman who could bring us victory, as our hope; as our protector of the east.

At first I was certain Shapur was contemplating keeping the peace he had agreed with Zenobia as he paused for many days on the outskirts of the city of Edessa. Odenathus and Ballista did not wish to wage our smaller forces against them yet. Our armies must wait. We needed to hold back until we had the advantage, and it was Zabbai who found it.

The Persian army began to move, though something told us they were not falling back to their own lands, or pushing further into Roman lands; they were heading south. The south only held two things for them: the Euphrates and, beyond the river, the largest eastern city they had yet to conquer, the city so nearly given to them by Valerian, Odenathus' city of marble: the south held Palmyra.

Zabbai knew the area well. He had defended these territories with the young prince Herodes for many years.

'The Persians are travelling south on the west leg of the Euphrates,' he said.

I packed away tents beneath a sweltering morning heat.

'And us, what are we to do?'

'We will travel on the east.'

Our combined armies set out the following daybreak, our shadows stretching long across the plain beyond the city. We left a small garrison at Edessa and travelled as fast as our baggage trains would allow. We took limited supplies in the hope that the supply chain previously arranged with Palmyra held, and that we would find food and provision in the days to come. We needed to cut the Persians off before they reached the desert plains in order to defend our city; our home. It was then, as we marched, heading toward home, toward the Persian army, that I felt the sense of return so familiar from mine and Zenobia's journey back from Rome. I could not wait to see Palmyra, and with that longing came thoughts of Julius and how much I missed him, how I hoped to see him again soon as I had seen him so briefly at Zenobia's marriage to Odenathus. Surely now, after so long, he might return home indefinitely?

The march proved hot. We Syrians sweated beneath our light armour, and the heat was even harder on the Roman soldiers who had come unprepared for the desert, clad in their iron and steel and padded tunics. But Ballista agreed with Odenathus; they would have the centurions press the men on remorselessly, without stopping, without rest. We all knew Palmyra could not fall, for if she fell so would the east and the supply of grain from Egypt to Rome.

When we finally crossed the river my will to stop the Persians, and my fear of not being able to do so in time, quelled the tiredness and hunger I felt. Provisions were near gone, but we made it before them: the Persians were nowhere in sight. Scouts returned to inform us that they were still on the move, coming slowly from the north, raiding along the way.

'I only pray they do not know we have also moved south,' Zabbai said to me as we made camp once more. I was adept now at constructing quickly the long, low black tents of our people, and talked as I worked.

'You think we can still surprise them?'

'If they believe that we think there is peace, then perhaps we can still surprise them.' He cuffed me fondly round the head and I punched his arm back.

Nearby, Zenobia laughed. She had marched on foot with me all day, despite the pack train carrying supplies and heavy cavalry with the Romans. Odenathus, back in command and frequently attending councils of war and meetings with Ballista, had not walked with us.

She sat cross-legged next to a hastily made camp fire. Leaning back on her arms, she allowed her head to fall back, looking up at the starry night. We should have been with the king, with his own personal guard, but Odenathus seemed not to care whose company she kept or her whereabouts, and she walked freely amongst the units with me by her side.

I sat down beside her.

'When do you think they will come?'

'Tomorrow,' Zenobia replied, unmoving.

'How do you know?' Zabbai and I both asked together.

She let her head fall further back and closed her eyes briefly.

'The goddess Selene is always with me. They will come tomorrow.'

'Tomorrow, the day after, the day after that. What does it matter? They come when they come,' Zabbai said.

Aurelia approached. She was as pale as ever, her golden hair cascading down her back, as if sunlit even though the sun had dropped. She sat down beside me and put a hand on my knee.

'I would pray they never come,' she said, and smiled so affectionately that I wished for a moment that she were right, that we could escape the battle we faced.

Zabbai eased off his shoes and said, 'Odenathus has ordered that you stay with Zenobia, Zabdas. You will be positioned with a guard well behind our lines. Shapur will be seething when he discovers we have cut him off from Palmyra, and if he should win the battle, and he should find Zenobia ... do not let that happen, understand?'

Distracted, I did not answer as I saw Odenathus walk down the lines of tents, speaking to his men, giving orders, ensuring all was well. He glanced at Zenobia more than once. I prodded the embers of our fire, recalling Odenathus' confession that Julius had made him swear to keep myself and Zenobia from harm. I had told Zenobia of this, and though she attempted to reassure me that she knew nothing of the promise, she seemed unsurprised.

With Zenobia's assurance of our enemy's arrival the following day, we dispersed as the fire's orange flames faded to a subtle glow. I did not sleep, lying awake throughout the night, my body tired but my mind fully awake, my restlessness owed to thoughts of the promise between Odenathus and Julius, the marital feud between the king and his queen, and because I was fearful of the Persians coming to face us for the first time on open ground.

Our legions were swollen with auxiliary troops, but we were far fewer in number than our enemy. I thought about it so much my head felt heavy and even closing my eyes did nothing to lessen the ache. Behind me, arms curled about me, Aurelia's warm body pressed against mine and she whispered that I should sleep.

Sleep, I thought. How I wished it would find me.

CHAPTER 14

Zabdas – 260 AD

Morning came and our scouts returned to camp. They informed us the enemy were close, moving at a steady pace, and would indeed arrive this day. I readied myself with a trembling heart. The centuries were in formation by mid-morning; determined to gain every advantage possible. The women, the old and the sick were behind us with our carts. I hoped the Persians would not break through our force and reach them. I dared not think what would happen to Aurelia if they did and prayed to the gods that our enemy would be tired and weakened from their long march south; that we had been blessed with a full night's sleep even though I had barely closed my eyes.

We stood on the plain. Thirty thousand men; those remaining of the seventy thousand we had once been when Emperor Valerian first came to Syria. The Persians we faced numbered more than one hundred thousand. The fear of my fellow warriors swelled the air around me. I felt my own fear, nervous and with a keen edge.

I was mounted on a camel beside Odenathus as messengers came to and fro, relaying the words of Ballista and the other commanders. Heavy plate armour covered his chest, over which a thick crimson cloak flicked in the breeze. Beside me an infantryman carried the king's helmet beneath his arm.

'Keep Zenobia from the battle, Zabdas,' Odenathus said as

he gestured to two commanders. 'Stay with her and let no harm come to her. If we are defeated this day, ride hard south to her father. Take her to Julius and tell him I have fallen and the armies of Syria have been defeated. Tell him I am sorry for everything that has passed between us, and that I owe him a great deal.'

'It will not come to that, my Lord.'

My hands shook and were clammy with sweat. I gripped the camel's reins tighter. The king's own horse agitated.

With the Emperor taken captive, the morale of the Roman force was low, despite the efforts of Ballista to rally the men beneath him. They had been hit with the humiliation of their emperor's captivity, and were unable to find sufficient faith in their new leader. It would take time to earn their trust and respect.

Odenathus rode to the head of the army as, stilled by his arm, a group of messengers and I hung back. The king, powerful and confident on his Arabian warhorse, moved from side to side before the men. For a moment I thought him a god, but only for a moment. My attention turned as a cheer rose from the Roman cohorts for the first time, along with an almighty roar from the Syrian ranks. The men began to bang spear and sword on shield.

I saw her then. From between the cohorts came Zenobia. She could be called a goddess, so her beauty shone and so the posture she held commanded. She appeared impenetrable to the sharpest blade and the heaviest sword.

She wore a simple robe of transparent silk. Her hair hung down her back, a great cascade of black curls. There were no jewels upon her person, no fineries of the east of any kind. As she reached the front of the gathered army, she turned the armoured horse and faced us. I could see now that her silks hung loosely upon her frame, and fell to reveal her left breast, proving to the gathered men that she was indeed a woman; that she would bring them victory.

She held the gaze of those before her as silence fell. There was no humour in her face now, no trace of the drunken flirtation of the previous nights in camp.

'I returned from the Persian camp,' she said, her voice in harmony with the breeze. 'I returned from King Shapur himself untouched, unharmed. I am a woman, but a woman who is blessed by the gods, by Selene. And they are all here with us this day.'

She paused, and the army was quieter than ever.

'The enemy that face us threaten the empire we are sworn to protect. I have met their king and he is weak. He cares only for plunder and rape and raiding. He wants our riches and our women. He does not want to rule our people, but to crush them beneath his greed. He would take every life here without mercy, without care, the same as he took captive our emperor, Valerian Caesar.

'I knew a man once; a man loyal to Rome. A man who gave everything to protect the empire he was born to serve. He had beliefs. He had pride. He gave an oath.'

Her words were carried back through the ranks and she surveyed the modest army before her.

'He had honour.'

A cheer rose, until shouts of who this man was carried forward, back through the ranks of warriors, back to Zenobia. Some yelled that it was Valerian, others that Gallienus was the man spoken so proudly of. But I knew.

'You have the fortune of fighting beside this man today.' She thrust her arm in the direction of Odenathus. 'The King of Palmyra was a soldier, like each and every one of you. He fights for you and with you. He has kept the Persian scum at bay. He kept them at bay for the empire he serves, for *her* people and for *his* people. Help him today. Help him rid our lands of the enemy …'

The army erupted in cheers and I too shouted my agreement, that I too would rid of us our enemies.

Zenobia raised her right arm and punched the sky.

'For the Empire,' she shouted.

'For the Empire,' the troops shouted back. All down the lines the echo of her words rippled.

'For *Rome*.'

'For Rome,' the echo replied.

'For Emperor Gallienus!'

More cheers of support rang out. Zenobia's face was alive. Upon her horse she sat straight and tall, surveying the men littered across the plain. I looked at her and I realised my own excitement and fear and above all my captivation with this girl who could rally such excitement from the men about to face battle.

For a moment I had forgotten what it was to risk my life, that a horde of Persians were headed toward us; that I would likely die on these sands and never again see the moon in the sky, never see the beauty of the stars or my sweet Aurelia's face again. I would be behind the army with Zenobia, but what would stop them? Could I truly outrun the charging Persians and see the south if the worst came?

As the chanting died I saw only thin lines of infantry that would tear apart when the enemy hit.

Zenobia edged her horse nearer to Odenathus and mouthed something. No one would have been able to hear what she said, just as I could not, but I knew what passed between them. She had said: 'For Palmyra and for Syria.'

I expected rage to contort Odenathus' features. She had defied him. She had lied to him. She was a traitor to Rome. But then he nodded, almost imperceptibly, and closed his eyes as if in thanks. He stood before the Persians, one force against another, and finally the day had come when he could fight to the last.

Behind the king and queen of Palmyra, great plumes of sand filled the air. I felt cold dread. A moment later, the horizon filled with a hundred thousand Persian warriors.

CHAPTER 15

Zabdas – 290 AD (Present day)

WE SAIL IN THE dark, the breeze cold and the moonlight shining on the water. There are no clouds these past few days, and little to hinder our progress downriver.

Samira is asleep now in the cabin with my men. She does not wish to sleep alone, and I cannot blame her for that. My men will watch over her and no harm shall befall her, I promise myself.

I stand now hunched, looking over the deck and the rippling sails. I ponder everything I had said so far and everything I needed to say. I will take Samira to Rome, to a place where she has never been before, and she will know the wonders of that city.

This was her father's wish, arranged since her birth, another promise I must keep, I think, and realise I will never be free of my oaths and my promises, always in my own debt.

Samira has asked me many times where her father comes into the tale, and each time I remind her that he was much younger than me. In our tale he has not yet been born. And whenever she asks guilt consumes me. Vaballathus had been a young man full of determination and clear vision. He knew what he wanted to achieve, and he could hold the desire for revenge with a burning passion. And as much as I am content in Bamdad's company as he guides the ship in the night, I cannot help but wish Vaballathus was still amongst us. I miss his jokes and his wide, white smile that brought his face alive. He was daring, a man who walked with purpose, someone who took risks and reaped reward.

But his last risk had seen him fail just as I had seen others fail before him. He had bargained everything for the greatest prize. He gave his life for the chance to kill our enemy.

Bamdad joins me and I sense his concern, the furrow in his brow and the words on his lips that he will not speak.

'You should get some rest,' he says.

I think of it, of closing my eyes and letting sleep take me. I have not slept fully in days. A flicker of light on the horizon and a feeling of being watched disturbs me more than I dared voice.

'You have noticed it too,' he says, following my gaze.

'What have I noticed?' I ask, unwilling to confess my unease.

'We're being followed. That is why you insist we sail day and night.'

He scours the horizon then glances at me. I hold my silence. There is little point in answering him, he knows me too well. I think perhaps my senses prickle with the knowledge that someone is always out there, always seeking, and now I know it is not only me, but that Bamdad feels it too.

'The Tanukh will not forgive us lightly for Jadhima's death,' he adds.

He speaks what I dare not voice. I wish the gods would not play with us, see us battle for their amusement. Jadhima was right, I think, there would always be a revenge to exact, because there is always someone left to desire that revenge, and I know already there is a price on my head. But I do not wish to stand again, to fight them, not with Samira aboard. I have chased the Tanukh for so long, it is strange to think that they now chase us.

'They cannot forgive us lightly, no,' I agree. 'You and I both know Amr will not forget the death of his uncle.' I rolled my shoulders. 'He was a savage when he was young, and Jadhima's kingdom will pass to him now.'

I can smell the day creeping upon the night. Feel the light about to emerge on the horizon. If the Tanukh were out for our blood, if others in search of the price on my head hunt us, we

Zabdas - 290 AD (Present day)

will know soon enough, and we will be ready for them. I sense rather than feel the weight of steel at my side, for I am used to it now.

Samira appears on the deck. I do not realise how long I have stood with Bamdad, lost in my thoughts, staring at shadows on the shore. Bamdad winks at her and she grins in return and I sense the bond they share, and know that he is as much a grandfather to her as I am. Sometimes I can feel a fragment of jealousy creep upon me, that he so easily captures her affections when I think to work so hard to be close to her, to protect her, and for her to trust me in return. It feels unnatural, as if I am a stranger and I have not been a part of her life since she was born.

Samira has become ever more intrigued by Bamdad since hearing of his participation in our tale, and yearns for more. He is growing old; many years have passed since we stood side by side as brothers and faced the Persians at Antioch. Where once his hair was black as coal, now it is greying, the years of battle taking their toll. And still his smile is young and mischievous, rather like Samira's.

My own bones ache in the cold wind as I think of how much time has passed since I first encountered my loyal friend. How the distances we have travelled and the choices we have made define us. I have become increasingly philosophical, I think, and to my amusement I think of Julius and I can but smile to myself that I should have now his traits even though I am not of his blood, but of Meskenit's. I wonder do all men seek philosophy as they progress in years. Bamdad, it seems, does not.

'I love the morning,' Samira says as she joins me.

'A fresh day full of new opportunities,' I reply.

She smiles; an innocent, fresh expression, one that I have seen on her many times, one that I remember seeing on Zenobia on in her early years.

'It is,' she says. 'Have we travelled far during the night?'

'We have made good time.' Bamdad winks again, and there is an awkwardness in Samira, as if something has passed between them, but I do not know what.

'We will reach Hama shortly,' I add, and take a deep breath. 'Then we travel to Antioch on foot, then the open sea.'

She smiles and leaves us, and I am once again alone with Bamdad.

'What has passed between you?' I ask him. I am not one for games. I am too old for them.

'Ah, Zabdas, you need to open your eyes. Have you any idea what she's feeling? Poor girl's had more to contend with these past days than you and I have in twenty years. Vaballathus is dead. He's not coming back. She knows this. She's weary with mourning him but you don't see it.'

I am taken aback by his words, and realise he is angry. Perhaps he is angry that I have not taken more care, that we should have stopped Vaballathus, or simply that he does not wish to see her hurting. I think the latter likely.

'You are right,' I say. 'She is hurting. The gods know I wish she was not.'

'Take a care with her. She's strong, but I do not think she's as strong as you like to think. She is no Zenobia.'

He is right once more. She is no Zenobia, but neither would I have her be. She is her own person, a young girl becoming a woman, and I would have a path for her that is safe, that does not hold danger, but every imaginable possibility that she could wish to choose from.

'No one will ever come close,' I say.

'I've read your documentation of what happened.'

'What of it?'

He does not speak, but shakes his head and laughs a little and walks away.

And I am left with that look, and wonder what it is that amuses him, which part of the tale he thinks a jest, what events he believes are not told as they should be. But they are my own recollections, my knowledge of that time, not his, and that is the one I am writing.

CHAPTER 16

Zabdas – 260 AD

Surrounded by soldiers, I felt oddly alone. Zenobia's horse moved nervously as she and Odenathus surveyed the army amassing before us on the hot and humid horizon. Zabbai rode up and down our lines of men, shouting orders, speaking encouragement, sending messengers back and forth.

I sat upon my camel, no familiar faces around me, watching as the workings of the army turned and moved and rotated. And I wished Zenobia would move back with me, back behind the lines of men where we had been instructed to be before the armies clashed.

I was between two cohorts in the central force. Sweat stung my eyes. I wiped it aggressively with my palms, making it worse, and feared that I would be unable to see when the enemy attacked. The ground here was uneven; chosen by Pouja because the Persians had more horses than we did, and it would serve to immobilize them, giving us the opportunity to attack and lever a small advantage.

Behind me the wind blew, cooling my neck, dragging with it a blanket of dust from the banks of the Euphrates.

'Stand firm. Today we fight for our countries. Today … we fight … FOR ROME!' I could just make out the Latin words bellowed to the Roman legionaries. Perhaps by Ballista himself, but I was too deep in the Syrian ranks to see.

Zabbai walked in front of the cohort nearest me and shouted, 'Warriors of the East, brothers and countrymen, remember this: we are all that stands between the Persians and invasion of the Roman Empire. We have been their shield. We have been their sword arm. We have been the slave that wipes the arse of Rome!'

We laughed and cheered, and for a moment my fear was forgotten. The words were not the words of Zabbai, although he spoke them, they were the words of a man who knew how to perform, how to rally his men when he needed to. They were the words of a general.

'And yet today we fight for more than Rome. We will see the Persians defeated. We will see them crushed into the ground, their blood staining our sands. And we will do it for ourselves, for our own country, for one another, because without each other we are nothing. Without each other, fighting side by side, we cannot protect this country or our homes or our families or our livelihoods. Remember that. Be sure we have victory, and let the Roman bastards know who saved them!'

A roar of support followed Zabbai's words as he carried on down the lines of men, repeating them over and again, spurring the men on, until all I could hear was a roar of noise in response.

The commands and speeches of encouragement continued as Odenathus and Zenobia pulled back, a contingent of commanding officers and messengers in their wake. I followed. Legionaries looked up at the king as he passed. If his eyes were upon them, their courage and skill in battle could be seen and rewarded.

But not for me, I would stay with Zenobia. I would not fight nor see the skills I had acquired used only as a guard for the eastern queen. But that did not seem to matter anymore. My frustration was quelled by the knowledge that it was because of the protection of Julius and that I could not imagine being anywhere but at Zenobia's side as the lines of Roman soldiers and the lines of Persian soldiers met. I would protect her, no matter what, and the thought of riding hard for the south, taking Zenobia to her father, filled my vision. Pray that does not happen.

Once behind the lines, Zenobia, her guard and I rode further back, beyond the reserve line from where we would observe the battle. I could see the formation of our men more clearly. Heavy infantry carrying spear and sword and shield were backed by a single rank of archers. Legates behind them were mounted on horseback. Flags fluttered overhead and I thought perhaps I saw light flickering on the legions' eagles, but I could not be sure.

'Odenathus stands too close to the fighting line,' Zenobia said.

I looked for the king's red cloak beyond the re-enforcements, amid the messengers and commanding officers sprawling the rear of our troops.

'Do not worry,' I replied. 'He knows what he is doing.'

Zenobia remained silent and continued to stare at our men.

I worried for her. She thought the king too close to the fighting line, when we were so close ourselves. I could have seen her further back. I thought perhaps to ride now for Julius and wait to be called before returning to Palmyra, but it seemed that all my senses were fixated on the army before us.

Seeing the lines forming on Zenobia's brow I said, 'What troubles you?'

'We have the best possible men commanding the Roman and Syrian armies. We have the most skilled legionaries in the world filling our ranks.' She met my eyes. 'But we are so very small compared to the Persian force. I do not fear for myself, standing here, I fear for our country. If we lose this battle, we lose Palmyra and the East. This is our chance to save it, to push back Shapur, to gain a defeat at last, and if we do not I think we will never recover from it. What are you thinking, Zabdas?'

After a moment I grinned half-heartedly.

'That I have never seen so many men in one place.'

In a haze of men and horses and heat, the enemy loomed ever larger. Soon individual riders could be made out amongst the swarm of warriors heading toward our lines. The enemy appeared greater in number than it had before, and I felt my own grip tighten on the sword at my hip, knotting the muscle in my forearm.

Persian kettle drums beat their awful rhythm. Zenobia and I could only watch as they neared. From the midst of churning dust, a lone rider pulled ahead of the Persian force.

The horse galloped frantically and the rider raised his right arm signalling he carried word from his masters. Odenathus bellowed a command from behind the line of archers backing the infantry, and a moment later arrows whistled overhead, thudding into the messenger, hitting him with such force he was thrown from his horse.

What message he carried from the enemy we would never know.

That was our reply to Shapur: the time for talk was over.

Drums beat.

Out of arrow range, the main Persian force came to a halt.

The entire plain fell quiet but for the sound of the guards next to me breathing heavily, the wind whistling at my back, and the rustle of armour and horses. Even the daunting beat of the kettle drums ceased. Grim-faced, the two armies watched one another. Halfway between, the Persian messenger lay dead, arrows protruding from his fallen body and his horse meandering aimlessly a few feet away.

More than one hundred and thirty thousand men stood on the plain; there were women too in the Persian ranks. Romans, Syrians, Persians; all moved simultaneously toward each other. Drums beat once more with the promise of blood and death, victory and defeat. Many would not see tomorrow. I could hear nothing but the battle cry of my people. *My* people. I was behind the fighting line, but for every part of me that was thankful, there was a bigger part that wanted to be in combat beside my countrymen. I wanted to be with them, help them, or die as one of them. I was torn between the joining the ranks and staying with Zenobia and taking her to greater safety. And for the first time since the Romans had come in force to Syria, I appreciated their presence.

Horns sounded as the front lines of both armies drew close to one another. Arrows hummed overhead and thudded into Persian shields and flesh and earth and horses, or else glanced off armour. More arrows flew. Soon the Persians were returning our arrow fire with their own waves of steel-tipped death until missiles broke apart their formation.

As the Persians advanced, so our own ranks moved forward. The two front lines met for what seemed like a heartbeat, before pulling apart. They moved toward each other again and there was a brief clash of metal followed by screams from the injured and the dying. I could not breathe and I could barely think. I kept looking to Zenobia, as if she would say something to ease my worries, but she looked on with a hardened expression, no surprise or worry or panic in her features. She betrayed nothing.

The Persians pushed hard into our left flank, and all I could do was watch. I scanned the rear line. Despatch riders with feathers tied to their spears moved back and forth. Whole cohorts rippled as they engaged the enemy. More arrows rained down on our men.

Behind the central formation, Odenathus waved his arm overhead, commanding officers and couriers and shouting support, spurring on his men, guiding them. The battlefield was his stage, the legionaries before him players. He moved back and forth, presumably to gauge the progress of his centuries more clearly.

Suddenly his horse began to meander away from the line. Odenathus arm dropped to his side, and his cloak lifted as he slid heavily from the horse and into the churning dust. There he lay and did not move, an arrow sticking vertically from his torso.

The king had fallen.

Beside me I heard Zenobia gasp, a whimper of distress

almost, then more shouts and more screams rushed across the ground to us and I was deafened by it.

A commander moved into Odenathus' position as a group of soldiers encircled their king. Men swept in from behind our lines and a moment later the king was carried away. The sound from the battlefield grew, and I suspected the Persians knew that our king had fallen, that one of our leaders no longer rallied his men, and that our Syrian ranks were weakened.

And my heart plunged at the sight of our first heavy loss.

'My Queen,' one of our company said, 'we need to move back.'

The guard said what I should have done, albeit in a nervous, fretful voice. He worried as I did I am sure that more losses would succeed the first. That the Persians would be rallied by the fall of our king and our troops would lose courage. Zenobia must move to safer ground. Odenathus would want that.

'My Lady?' the guard persisted. 'My Queen? ... Zenobia? We must move back to safety. The king was specific …'

His voice trailed off as Zenobia shook her head. Her face pale and her eyes empty she spoke in a calm voice. 'Go back and get the baggage train moving toward the city. Make sure our people reach safety. Get them inside the walls. Our king has fallen, but we will not lose this fight. We cannot lose this battle.'

There was no time to argue as she spurred her horse across the sands toward our army.

'Zenobia!' I called after her. Then instinctively I followed, my camel's speed closing the gap between us.

The noise intensified as we neared the battle and the two beasts came to a halt behind the rear rank. I was not prepared for this. The noise was more deafening that before, and I could barely hear my own voice as I called after her. We were so close to the killing that I could smell the blood and sweat and shit of the dying and dead.

Zenobia and I moved across to where the heavily armoured, mounted commander bellowed orders. Pouja looked at us then looked again.

'Get out of here now. You are a target for the enemy, get back,' he shouted to Zenobia. Then to a courier: 'Have reserves brought up on the left flank before the Persian cavalry punch a fucking hole in our line.'

But they were staring at Zenobia. In frustration he turned back to her and said, 'I told you to get back. Get out of here. This is no place for you.'

'The soldiers should see that their queen is amongst them.'

'Odenathus will have my fucking head!' he growled back.

'King Odenathus has fallen,' Zenobia replied, her tone matter of fact. 'And the morale of our troops will wane. You need me here.'

In fury Pouja turned away and instead looked at me for longer than was comfortable before saying, 'Zabdas, if you want to smell enemy shit then get off that camel, draw your sword, and join the fucking reserve. Do it now before I change my mind. Ha, change my mind,' he said more to himself. 'I always thought Odenathus should control his woman better but it seems no one can.'

In the confusion that followed, I did as I was told, leaving Zenobia at the commander's side. The enemy and Roman lines were not engaged as I joined the central reserve, but instead shouted insults to one another. Nothing was in perspective; every sense heightened by what was happening and would come. The smell of sweat ridden leather filled my nostrils, polished iron gleamed, and the sound of thirty thousand men ready for battle deafened me. In that moment I wondered why I was here. Why I stood amidst the armies of the Roman Empire, amongst men of many countries, waiting to fight an enemy. And then I knew. I stood waiting to face men who would invade the country I had come to love. In my army were people I cared for. I fought amongst friends; amongst people who saw me as one of them. I belonged here, as a warrior. I belonged with Zenobia. And I would fight and I would die here if it meant I was a part of it.

'You ready for a fight?' a familiar voice shouted to my right.

I looked around to see Bamdad, wild-eyed, just as he had been at the gates of Antioch.

'I am,' I replied, relishing the fact that suddenly my fear had gone, replaced by an ecstasy I could not even begin to explain. Bamdad was here and the thought of our previous fight together came to me with the notion that this was just the same. We stood before the enemy once more. We had survived.

Bamdad held my gaze and grinned.

I must have been as wild-eyed as he in that moment. I grinned back. I had not expected to be here and held no spear. I gripped my sword and shield tight. The words, 'Are you ready,' went unsaid, as we both turned to face the enemy.

And both our line and the Persian line advanced.

My breathing came deep and urgent, knowing there would be no turning back, but simultaneously knowing I did not want to. I could no longer hear words or individual shouts. My ears were filled with the mingled noise of two armies waiting to face each other. Of drum beats, shouting, cursing, growling, sword and spear rapping on shield and foot-stamping on the dusty, piss-soaked earth.

The men in front of me crashed into the disordered enemy ranks, lapping them, the clatter of iron like the froth of waves, relentless water on rocks; the heat like the sun on the baking earth; the fear like nothing I had felt before.

My thirst for death was a familiar desire.

We became crushed, squashed up against the enemy. Either side of me soldiers thrust spears over the heads of those in front. But I had no spear, only a sword. Men before me fell, and the Persians scrambled over them and I thrust and cut and sliced and struck in desperation because I did not want to die, but most of all because I felt the urge to kill. My veins were lava-blood and I wanted to spill that of the enemy before me.

But the Persian scum must have known that same drive and

desire. They pushed hard into us. I heard men shriek with pain as their limbs were sliced and their lives drained to the Otherworld. I found slaughter with a furious need to protect myself and those around me. I no longer thought. My whole being surged on of its own accord, not knowing, not planning, but acting on my years of training and the instinct warriors know.

Our lines separated once more, leaving the debris of battle screaming for death between us. I gasped for breath. There was no one in front of me now. I had become the front line. Behind me commanders urged us on. Meet the enemy running. And before I knew it we met again. I pushed up my shield, catching the helmet of a Persian and, with a grunt, I slid my sword under the rim and up into his skull. With a growl I pulled it free. I caught sight of blood leaking from beneath before I climbed over the fallen and moved on. I killed again and again, but around me more and more of our own fell. And with that knowledge my desire turned to desperation. I hacked and clawed and cut and killed.

I heard screaming, then realised it was my own as I sliced over and over at an already dead enemy. Someone shouted my name, and I knew it was Bamdad who pulled me from that place. The two lines broke apart and he gestured to our left. It was breaking; Persian bastards pushing beyond our line, punching a hole deep into our shallow ranks. Bamdad shouted again, but I could not hear. I howled a battle cry as the enemy scrambled over the dead toward me and we were engaged once more.

Blood, a tide of it, sprayed everywhere, with ribboned flesh and shards of armour falling to the already soaked earth. I was close enough to kiss the enemy, to feel their putrid breath on my face and taste their stench on my lips and tongue. I thought of every person they had killed, every family they had broken, every husband torn from his wife and father taken from his children. I thought of the country and my duty and that this was our last chance. Fall now and we would never rise again.

There was so much to pay for, and I would force a reckoning.

My arms tired. I knew they did because my mind told me so, but I did not feel it, did not succumb to the aftermath a soldier feels when the enemy are all dead, because they were not. They pushed and drove into us. They slaughtered us. They annihilated our flank and they tore out our very hearts. All the while I remained determined to kill; just kill. I growled. I bared my teeth. I learned that the enemy were the same; men, just like us, or flesh and blood and mortal bones. Yet still I took their lives with ease. Still I leant on my sword and watched men slip from this life.

And then I took a woman. She shrieked; louder and more chilling than any man. Her face wild and her hair untamed and her eyes, filled with mad-rage, looked at the shadow of me. She came at me with her hands, her claws, and a knife, too. Her bare arms were covered in dirt and grime. She screamed as she leapt at me, but she did not get close before I cut her down without remorse.

'Keep together. Close up, close up.'

'They are not to get through. Push hard, men.'

'Advance!'

'Kill them! Skewer the fatherless sons of whores and send them to a Christian hell.'

'The gods are with us!'

'You are Roman, you are the elite of warriors.'

'The Persians are already dead.'

The commands and encouragement shouted by the Roman officers was heard despite the battle-noise. Either side of me soldiers butted their shields tight together and we stood fast. The Persian line, climbing over both their dead and ours, thudded into us, and the sound of iron and the shrieks of the dying filled my mind.

Over everything I heard Zenobia's voice, piercing the growls of men. Or maybe I just imagined it. But it was followed by a roar from behind me, and I suspected more reserves came to add their weight.

'Zabdas!' Bamdad shouted.

I pushed my opponent back, but there were men behind him, pressing him onto me. We were so squashed neither one could kill the other, his acid breath licking my face. I chanced a glance right and saw our line crumple beneath the enemy's weight.

'Hold them. Fucking hold them! Gods damn them all, for we will win.'

'Don't let the damned filth get the better of you! Hold the fucking line!'

It was all I could hear, over and over again. Repeated and regurgitated.

'Hold them.'

'Hold the fucking line.'

I looked at Bamdad and saw his face contort with pain.

'NOOO!' I heard the word before I realised I had shouted.

Bamdad appeared to recover; his expression filled with rage and pain and bloodlust as he found his legs. There was no time to see what he did next. I felt our own men pressing behind me. In front, my shield trapped my arm to my chest, and with the other I lunged desperately. Suddenly, the weight seemed to disappear, and I fell forward, pushed by my countrymen. Falling onto the dead.

The two lines had broken apart again.

'Their flank has fallen!' a legate shouted from behind us.

'Kill them! Slaughter them all!'

Then I heard a female voice, Zenobia's voice.

'This is our day. The gods are with us.'

I felt the smallest relief as I cheered with the rest of our men, but I could not hear my own shout amidst the din.

I heard Zenobia's voice once more, urging us on, and made to engage again. Only this time the Persians appeared apprehensive. Howls rang from my right and our line moved forward. The enemy cried defiantly, but their advance was not as loud as before. They were losing heart, and I knew it.

Zenobia was right.

The Fate of an Emperor

The gods were on our side.

'Advance! Advance! Advance! They are not dead yet!'

'Bastards!' screamed a man to my left. 'Fucking bastards!'

A spear struck my shield and the weight dragged it from my grasp. I held my sword with both hands and bludgeoned the enemy. We could win. I just needed to survive. I realised I was still striking the man as he lay on the ground, his helmet crushed into his skull, and the enemy line had broken from ours.

But they had not just broken.

The ring of swords lessened. They were moving back. We followed; chasing them, killing them, slaughtering them, letting their blood onto the sands of Syria. And then tiredness overcame me. I shook. My legs gave way and I fell to the dark, stinking ground; my breath ragged and quick. I looked for Bamdad first. He simply stared at the retreating enemy, his face blank and his entire body drenched crimson. Then his sword slipped from his hand and he collapsed.

I tried to move across to him, to see if he was hurt, to try to help him if I could, but my legs would not carry me. Everywhere the injured moaned and cried and the living drew ragged breaths. I tried to comprehend all the lives I had taken, but every life taken blurred into the next, and I could not separate one death stroke from another. So many men. So many lives.

We had made a stand against the Persian tide.

And we had found victory.

CHAPTER 17

Zabdas – 260 AD

ZENOBIA SAT ON THE ground next to Odenathus' still form and watched him. We were in his low black tent, the light dim and the air sweet and medicinal herbs. I crouched beside him. Even now, despite his vulnerability, he was an impressive figure, his huge chest rising and falling and the scars of old battles shining like slug trails. Blood oozed through bandages smothering the wound where the arrow had found a weak gap in his armour.

'What have the physicians said?' I asked.

She shook her head, a gesture I did not understand, and smiled wanly.

'They are optimistic. We are to pray a few weeks will see him back to full strength. Herodes and Pouja left a little while ago.'

After the battle, Zenobia and I had made a hasty return to camp. Our victory had come about because of Zenobia's presence amongst the men. It had rallied their spirits, so I heard. She was their mascot, their queen and Selene's chosen one in our world. My fellow soldiers had sensed the Persians' fear at the sight of her.

I still trembled from the aftermath of battle. My senses were heightened and everything seemed so clear and raw.

'There is much to do now we have gained the advantage,' I said.

She nodded absently, her face full of sorrow, so different from the determination and strength she had shown as she supported the army and faced the enemy. She looked as tired as I felt and there was something in her eyes that I could not place. Then I saw a tear trace the contour of her cheek.

I had never considered that she loved Odenathus. I had always assumed her indifferent, that she had lain in his bed because she had to, because her marriage was desired by her father and by her, to breed the next ruler. Never had I thought that she truly wanted to be with the king for the man himself.

She did not wipe the tears away, but let them trickle down her face and onto Odenathus' hand, which was gripped by her own.

He had been in the midst of the battle; faced the same enemy and risked his life just as I had, just as she had. It was Zenobia's love for him, his having her, knowing her, that had caused my years of hatred. I had known her love for the king was there, right from the first, but I could never accept it. I had Aurelia now, and yet I still felt bitter and jealous of the tears she shed for him. He did not deserve a queen so strong. When she had lain close to death after the loss of their child, he had not stayed with her, watched over her, doted on her as I had; as she did for him now.

'I am with child again,' she said.

'I know you are.'

My words escaped my lips without thinking, without pause. I had known. I had seen the paleness in her complexion, had witnessed her willingness to obey Odenathus when he had ordered her back behind the reserve before battle, even though she had gone on to disobey him. Noticed her protective hand on her stomach, the change in her black pupils and the shine of her hair.

She tore her eyes away from her husband and looked at me with curiosity.

'I see it in your eyes. I recognise their appearance when you carry another life.'

Her expression softened and she smiled sadly.

'It feels as if you have always known me, Zabdas, long before my father brought you home.'

'I would like to think so.'

'Then you know I will not pursue Shapur's remaining force back to Persia with the army. I cannot risk it, nor can I bear the thought of the loss again. For the sake of the child, I will return to Palmyra and stay there until it is born. For once, I will do what Odenathus would want me to do. I will be safe enough so there will be no need for you to accompany me. I will speak to him when he wakes and ensure you can stay with the army. If the baby ... *when* the baby is born, I will call on you and perhaps my father will visit us both, or we can go south see him.'

'Gratitude, Zenobia, I would like that. You will be missed. I will miss you,' I said, knowing that I spoke for not only myself, but for both the Syrian army and the Roman legions and so many commanders in each. She had earned the respect of all.

'It is only for a short time, Zabdas.'

I had grown too used to her company. I wanted to stay with her, be close to her, but I also knew that I was her cousin and now I knew myself to be her half-brother, and I was a soldier and knew I could never have her for myself. I set my face with the same hard, cold look I had seen on hers so many times before.

'It is for the best.'

She stared at me a moment. Tears for the king still ran down her cheeks, but there was something else behind them, a different kind of hurt.

And then it was gone.

CHAPTER 18

Zabdas – 260 AD

IT TOOK ODENATHUS FOUR weeks to recover his strength. Even then I could see the weakness in his eyes, though he did not betray it physically. Our men recovered, too, both from the battle and the plague and sickness that had ravaged the army whilst in Edessa. More men came out of training and filled our ranks, and more tribes joined us too, knowing of our victory, determined not to lose out on any wealth that might be had, any reward from Rome or plunder retaken.

Zenobia returned to the sanctuary of Palmyra as her belly began to expand once more. To my relief, Aurelia went with her. Zenobia spoke with Odenathus as she had promised and I was permitted to stay with the army; as part of the king's personal guard this time, and not hers.

Our army rode on the elation of victory. We were savouring these lands being ours once more. And we grew healthy on it.

The campaign was hard as we made our way across ravaged lands in pursuit of Shapur and his remaining forces. Strong and determined, Odenathus spoke of pressing the enemy back beyond their own capital, beyond Ctesiphon.

For the first time in years, it seemed possible.

Our army camped to the east of the Euphrates, close to Edessa. We had not seen the enemy in three days, though we witnessed deserters choosing to settle in Syria. Some had found women to be with, to be close to, not to bed as slaves but to take as wives. Others preferring our trade routes and the profit that went with them.

We killed most and spiked their heads by the roadsides as we pushed further into territories we had not trodden in years; a lesson to those who thought to take our lands.

One morning, as the sun began to peak and our army hooted and laughed and were merry on the road, we came across a Persian who deliberately sought our army. He was encased in Persian armour and riding a horse, but now slumped on his knees before Odenathus, Zabbai, three other stratego and me. Beside him, Pouja clenched and unclenched his fists as he spoke.

'He had the nerve to ride into our camp. He must have known he would not live. Yet still he came.'

'Why did he come?' Odenathus asked.

The Persian looked up at us through bruised eyes.

'He delivers a message from Shapur,' Pouja replied.

'Why send one of his own when he knows he will not live?' I asked. 'The Persians have enough of our own countrymen taken as slaves, he could have sent any one of them.'

'He is demonstrating that he is not afraid,' Odenathus said. 'He wants to prove he has men enough to sacrifice; men with enough will to care nothing for death.'

I did not really understand, but I nodded nonetheless.

'What is the message?' Odenathus asked Pouja with a jerk of his head.

'He says he has seen Valerian Caesar in the Persian camp, my Lord. I think it best if you hear what he has to say for yourself.'

Odenathus paused for a moment, taking deep breaths. My own curiosity rose, and with it a sense of dread. Could Shapur be willing to return Valerian for a sum? Would the Romans discover this and know then of Zenobia's treason?

'He speaks Syrian?' Odenathus asked.

'Not that we know of.'

'Then get me a translator.'

An interpreter was fetched and Pouja said, 'Ballista and the Roman generals know nothing of this man. I brought him to you discreetly.'

The king nodded. 'That is probably wise. What is it he has to say?'

'I do not know, my Lord. He refuses to speak with anyone but you.'

The Persian began in his tongue, his face bruised and crusted in blood and dirt, he smiled as he spoke. And when he had finished, the translator began:

'We had not thought your emperor would come. We did not think him stupid enough to walk into the trap set by your queen. A boy was given to us, a boy my king believed your queen cared for, to secure the bargain, but still my king did not believe she would bring Valerian Caesar, Emperor of Rome.'

'I know this already,' Odenathus growled, and I realised then the prisoner did not recognise me as that same boy, and neither did I recognise him. This man was a messenger only, one who had not witnessed the treachery which he relayed.

The interpreter, concentration on his face continued as the Persian's message became more of a story, a narrative of the fate of an emperor:

'My king, Shapur, the first of his name, King of the Persians, King of Kings, King of the Sassanian Empire, did not kill Valerian Caesar immediately. He confined him to a cage of piss and shit and filth for two weeks. When finally Caesar was dragged from the cage he shouted and screamed like a woman.

'Our people gathered to watch. We took him to the tent of our great Shapur, and pushed him to the ground at the feet of our king, who sat, like a statue, unmoving; a greater man than any other.

'My lord asked him why he would betray his own people. He wanted to know why a Roman emperor would be betrayed by the Warrior Queen. She had said it was for peace, but Shapur did not believe her.

'But your emperor was confused. He thought it was a man who had betrayed him. You, King Odenathus, and not a woman.

'Shapur told Caesar that it was not King Odenathus who betrayed him, but the Warrior Queen, wife to Odenathus, the one of black hair and black eyes and pearl teeth. He looked at the pitiful form before him and said, "Women of Persia held respect for Roman emperors, but no more. Many say you are the greatest, most powerful man in the world. But how can you be, when you are so easily betrayed by a woman?"

'Life drained from your emperor's face but still his eyes flared with arrogance. Shapur was intrigued by your Warrior Queen. Something about her interested him. She showed no fear walking into our camp and addressed Shapur as an equal. Her forthrightness amused him. Saved her, even. She came to him with a bargain: the Roman emperor for the lives of her people. He had been right to trust her. She had delivered on her word and betrayed the Roman. But Shapur planned to march on Palmyra anyway ...'

Odenathus grunted with impatience.

'Shapur wanted to know more of the girl who had become a warrior queen, he wanted to know *who* she was, who her father was, what drove her ambition.

'Valerian Caesar said that he thought your queen's father a merchant and Shapur claimed she must be more than a merchant's daughter. She spoke with a force known only to those of power. And then he commanded Caesar to sit. Told him he was an emperor and should be treated as one, and so I fetched him a stool.

'In that very tent sat the two most powerful men in the world. Shapur followed his father, Ardashir, who built a strong empire. Rome is great, but she is falling. Persia will expand her borders to a far greater extent.

'Shapur wanted to know whether your emperor felt the power. Whether he had pride in his empire. Caesars are entrusted with millions of lives, more land than they can ever walk on. He wanted to know how it made Caesar feel.

'Your emperor's face fell blank of expression, and then he murmured that he wanted to make the Empire what she had been. He wanted to make her strong once more.

'Shapur asked why, and we waited to hear his words.

'Caesar replied that my king had said it himself. That Rome was once great and he wanted to restore her.

'Again Shapur asked why and Caesar cried out that it was because he wanted to be remembered.

'Shapur agreed. Leaders want to be remembered. They want to succeed and be remembered for that. More than simply a man who plunges a country, an empire, into chaos. They want to do great things and be remembered for them.

'The following day our army moved south and that evening your emperor was called to Shapur's presence one more. He sat on the same stool and peered into the face his captor as my king asked to know more of you, Odenathus. He wanted to know who would command Rome's eastern armies now their emperor was gone. Caesar snorted, held out his bound wrists, and demanded to be untied. Shapur replied that he would rather cut off his hands than untie them.'

The Persian must have expected some reaction from Odenathus, for he paused. But Odenathus stared at him impassively.

'Caesar claimed that his men would not follow you because you are a traitor. But they do not know, do they? The Romans do not know you Syrians betrayed their emperor?' The Persian laughed again. 'My king knew the Roman soldiers would not turn against you. He knew they had no idea you Syrians handed him to us. Your queen sat on the very same stool as your emperor when she promised Shapur his life.

'Your emperor said that the Warrior Queen was a traitor, and how could my king trust a traitor. But Shapur does not trust her, he never did. He only hoped she would keep her word. And Shapur realised your people were not exchanging the emperor's life for peace, but for something more. He wanted to know why the Warrior Queen really betrayed Caesar ... whether your emperor stood in the way of Odenathus' advancement. Either way, it did not matter, for the following day we would annihilate what remains of your forces. But we did not.

'Shapur was injured in the battle and suffered fever for many days before he woke. His son, our prince Barhram, did not think he would live; none of us did. He spoke of your Warrior Queen on her horse, a breast exposed for the soldiers to see that a woman rode amongst them. Her long dark hair trailing down her back to rest on her horse. He spoke of her over and over.

'Both my king and your Roman emperor were defeated by a woman; the same woman. The Warrior Queen had taken control of the armies of Rome and Syria.

'Shapur thought the Roman emperor weak, being betrayed by a woman and captured by his enemy; said he had disgraced the whole of Rome when he met my king on the plain. Rome: The Greatest Empire in the World,' the Persian spat. 'No. My king's empire, the Sassanian Empire, will be far greater!'

Pouja gave a short huff and instructed the Persian to continue.

'Shapur said he knew the warrior queen was clever, knew there was more to her, but he never believed her to be so capable. Not only had she turned traitor to Rome, she had led the Roman army to victory where the emperor could not. That is why he thought Valerian Caesar betrayed. Not because she thought to buy peace, but because he stood between her and victory.

'My king might have suffered defeat, but he has men enough to compile an army thrice over. He will still be remembered as the man who captured a Caesar. And so he gave my people your emperor's life.'

It took a moment before I realized what he said. Valerian: dead. I looked at the men around me. Pouja's face was set hard as he stared at the Persian captive. Zabbai glanced to Odenathus, worry in his expression. Odenathus scratched his bearded cheek.

The Persian looked at us, a manic grin spreading over his features.

'He pissed himself as we tied him to the frame,' he taunted. 'He pleaded for his life as we stripped him of his clothes.'

Odenathus took two long strides toward him and punched the Persian in the face. 'Is that your message? That is what you came here to tell me? That your king killed an emperor? Has he no respect?'

As Odenathus spoke the words, I looked around me at the Syrian generals and in each of their faces I saw the same regret, that we had needed to do what we had done to secure our victory, but none of us liked it, that there was no respect to be found in us either, the men who had handed Valerian over to Shapur.

Odenathus turned his back and the Persian hissed a stream of words. The translator looked petrified as Odenathus turned to him for a translation.

'He screamed as we stripped him of flesh.'

The Persian laughed. I felt only repulsion. It had occurred to me that Valerian would be dead, indeed everyone in our camp had rumoured that outcome, but to hear of his last days, knowing his demise had been secured with my own life, turned my stomach.

Pouja looked to Odenathus for response.

'Make sure he knows nothing else then kill him,' Odenathus said.

Pouja nodded as two soldiers dragged the Persian away.

'Then it is confirmed. One co-emperor is dead,' Zabbai mused.

'It would seem so,' Odenathus replied. He rubbed his knuckles and watched as the Persian laughed maniacally in the distance.

'What happens now?' I asked.

'Nothing,' Odenathus said. 'Gallienus is sole emperor. Ballista commands the Roman legionaries and we continue pushing the Persians back.'

'When the Romans discover Valerian is no longer a captive but a corpse, there could well be usurpers, and it could stem from here, in the east. Gallienus resides in the west ...' Zabbai noted, and even I heard the question in his voice. The question as to whether Odenathus himself would think to attempt usurpation.

'Then it is for us to make sure there are no usurpers,' Odenathus said. 'You are dismissed, Zabbai. I need a moment alone with Zabdas.'

'Of course.'

Odenathus and I had become closer during the time we had spent pressing the Persians back across the Euphrates. My position in the army had been elevated; I was one of the king's personal men and something of a confidante. He had warmed to me, I think. And my respect for him grew as I saw his command and authority of the eastern legions and his determination that we would not lose, we would not be pushed out of our own lands, and we would suffer no longer as we had done under the command of Valerian.

Since the battle, since I had seen Zenobia's love for him and finally accepted it, I felt I was working with him rather than against him for the first time.

'Walk with me.'

I obeyed and we began to stroll toward the edge of the camp.

'I must thank you,' he said, 'for your part in Zenobia's return to Palmyra. I understand it was you and Aurelia who persuaded her it was the best possible place for her and our child.'

His sudden gratitude surprised me. It had been months since Zenobia's return to the city. There had been many opportunities for him to speak of it. And even then it had been her own choice, needing no persuasion from me or anyone else.

'No, my lord, you are wrong. You know Zenobia cannot be easily persuaded. She went to Palmyra for yours and the child's sake alone; no other.'

'You are right, she cannot be easily persuaded. I of all people know that.'

Odenathus clasped his hands behind his back and looked out across the blank sands.

'A messenger arrived this morning, from Palmyra. Zenobia

has given birth to a son. To my son.'

I had expected the news eventually, indeed I had been known to look in the direction of the city some mornings, waiting for the rider who would bring the news, yet still I felt the hot lick of resentment.

I caught myself.

'That is most welcome news.'

'It is great news.' He smiled and I thought how I happy I would be when a child of my own came.

'They are both well?'

'I believe so. I tell you this, Zabdas, because I know Zenobia is a sister to you, and because she expressed a wish for you to travel back with me to Palmyra. I think maybe she misses being at the frontier, perhaps being with me, but I know she will be missing your friendship and your company a great deal. You have always been there for her when she needed you.'

'I think you are right, she will be missing the frontier most.'

We both laughed at that.

'The army and the influence she is capable of wielding, you mean?' he said.

I thought the words bitter, but his expression danced with amusement as he continued to look across the plain. All of this was his land. He had kingship, Roman legions bolstering his own Syrian forces, he had victory over the Persians, loyal Stratego and friends, a queen whose will was stronger than any other; and now he had another son. His kingdom was finally solidifying.

'Will Prince Herodes travel back with us?' I asked.

'He will not. Herodes I will leave in command of the army, here, alongside Zabbai and Pouja. The more Syrian generals I can keep in command the better at the moment. Ballista and the Roman generals are already talking of moving their legions. They are hard men to keep under control. It will just be us and a small escort returning to the city.' He breathed in deeply and looked down at me as I stared up at him. Even now, after I had grown into a man, still he towered above me.

'When do we leave?'

'Our frontier is secure. A visit home could not have come at a better time. We will leave at first light. I have missed my city. My home.'

CHAPTER 19

Samira – 290 AD (Present day)

'I KNOW YOU NEVER speak of it,' my grandfather says to Bamdad. 'But tell me something. When you killed Mareades all those years ago, did it bring you peace?'

Bamdad sighs and I see the raw hurt in his face, a flicker of what has gone before, and the memories he would rather shake.

'You have told Samira what happened?' Bamdad says, gesturing to me.

'You have read what I have told her,' Grandfather replies.

Bamdad shadows his eyes from the rising sun and looks at the horizon and then behind us, to the banks that move ever further away, and the places we have left behind.

'I found no peace in the death of that man,' Bamdad says. 'He was betrayed by the priest and by those who refused to believe him, and in turn he betrayed the whole city. My years are greater than yours, and still I find myself haunted. Still I feel loss; nothing will make it go away. Have you found peace now Jadhima is dead? I see you grimace at the mention of him, as if the pain should have disappeared, but it has not.'

I see the hurt in my grandfather's face, and I think something has passed between these two men, those who are my family.

'I thought I would,' Grandfather replies. 'I thought as his life ebbed from him, the pain would ebb from me. Nothing has changed; nothing but the fact that Vaballathus is no longer with us. I should have known. You know how many lives I have taken in revenge. This was no different. And it will never end.'

Bamdad shakes his head. It is as if the argument has gone out of him, as if he no longer wishes to speak heated words and dig up a past both would rather forget.

'Do not dwell on it,' he says, slapping his friend on his back and walking away. 'Perhaps if Amr finds us and wishes to take revenge for the death of his uncle, we can relieve some of our pain with a few more deaths to our blades?'

'When they are dead, I shall tell you.'

Grandfather does not look at me, as if he wishes I had not heard the words exchanged, the mention of my father, the regret and the pain he feels. He does not seem to realise that I feel it too. Time, I think, we need a little time for the memories to fade. It has only been a few weeks since I rode into Palmyra beside Bamdad, and my grandfather gave me the news of my father's passing.

'I can barely believe the Persians went back on their word,' I say to ease the silence. 'That they could think to march on Palmyra; that Shapur could turn against Zenobia after she had given them the emperor.'

'Zenobia never doubted they would.'

'And you won?'

'We won that battle, yes, and we won more. We were pushing them back, further and further. Our confidence grew, and we began to believe we could push them back beyond our original frontier.'

I think of Aurelia, sweet Aurelia, the girl who loved my grandfather so much that she would have done anything for him. That she waited months for his return, for the moments she would spend with him, and that he thought more of Zenobia than he did of her.

'Who did you love?' I ask, and I am surprised by my own blunt question. 'Zenobia or Aurelia?'

'I loved them both. Aurelia deserved more than I ever gave

her. I took her from Rome and I felt always guilty for that, because I could not give her everything, just as Julius could not give Meskenit as much as he wanted when he brought her to Palmyra from Egypt. I admit I loved Zenobia more than a sister; more than a queen. I doted on her, I wanted to be at her side, I was jealous of her husband and would have done anything she asked of me. But her desires and ambitions distanced her from everyone. And despite how close we became, I could not have her. No one could. She was well-born, married to the most powerful man in Syria, she had given birth to his child, and though it pained me every moment of every day, I set my desire aside, just as I always had.'

I cannot help but think of the love my grandfather had for her, and that it would never be returned. And I wonder did she love him at all. She must have done, I tell myself, for the reluctance she showed at leaving him in the Persian camp.

'And Julius loved you like a son,' I say. 'He must have been so proud of you. For everything you did.'

Grandfather smiles.

'When I think back, I hardly knew Julius. But through his beliefs, through Zenobia and his family and all who knew him, I felt I did. Zenobia's beauty might have been carved by the same tool as her mother's, but she was definitely her father's daughter, I have no doubt of that.'

He turns and looks back upriver and I know that tears sting his eyes.

The next day I find my grandfather and Rostram talking. We approach Hama and we can move no further along the river. We must continue on foot or camel and wind our way towards Antioch.

'If that is what you want,' I hear my grandfather say.

'It is the advantage, my friend, of being a free man who can do as he likes,' Rostram replies.

'Then so be it.'

Grandfather leaves, touching my arm as he does so, and I hear him bellow across the deck to Bamdad.

I am left four paces from Rostram, and he looks at me and nods in acknowledgement but says nothing.

I look around the boat, awkward and uncomfortable and thinking that I might turn and walk away as if I had never approached, as if I had not come to speak with my grandfather, as if he had not brushed past me to talk with Bamdad. I can think only of Bamdad holding me as I wept, of the tears that stung my eyes and the loneliness I felt, and that I had wished it was Rostram and I do not know why.

'I will miss this boat,' I say, looking about me, for something to say rather than because the words are true. In fact I will not miss it, the stench of slavery and the rotting wood. I will be glad to have two feet upon the land once more. To feel the ground and to know that it does not move beneath me.

'You may wish you were still aboard but I will not,' he says, and sits upon a crate, hands clasped before him and elbows on his knees, and through squinted eyes he looks about us.

'You will not?' I ask, confused.

'That is what your grandfather and I discussed. I am selling this boat.'

'Oh.' I am unsure what else to say, what more I can speak. 'You will buy another?'

'Once we reach the sea. Your grandfather is pleased. He thinks it is time that I ceased trading in slaves and began trading in goods.'

'I think he is right,' I say, and I can feel myself nodding, the reprimand in my voice. And then I realise what he has said, that he will buy a ship when he reaches the Mediterranean.

'You will journey with us?' I say.

'A shipload of cargo will make a tidy sum in Rome,' he says. 'And someone has to watch over you. Zabdas has done a poor job of that so far.'

Zabdas - 290 AD (Present day)

He glances up at me and I think perhaps there is a smile on his lips but it is faint and I know that he is taking pleasure from his words, and that he wishes to taunt me.

'And yet you came to our rescue,' I reply, 'because you are a slave-trader.'

'All men must work. Only Zabdas believes that defending a city long since dead, martyring oneself to a useless cause, and slaughtering ancient enemies is work.'

'He did not slaughter him,' I reply, my head high and my words choking in defence. 'He took revenge.'

Am I understanding now I wonder, what it is to take revenge? Or am I simply offended that this man, this Rostram, a slave-trader, would call my grandfather a slaughterer of men?

'Bamdad tells me you look like your grandmother,' he says.

'I did not know either of them.'

For moment I wish I had, that they had not died a long time ago, that they were here and that I might see them and know where I came from, that there might be a woman in a life so full of men and sweat and leather and steel.

Rostram shrugs as if matters little. I am resentful of that gesture, of his brushing away the mention of someone I have never known, that I might never want to know them nor wonder at the people they were.

I know my eyes are narrow as I look out at the fertile land beyond our boat; at farms and fields and irrigated crops.

EPILOGUE

Zabdas – 260 AD

How I had craved Palmyra. I smiled at the familiar sights and smells as we entered the city. By the gods, but it was just how I remembered it. I wanted to go to the temple and pray to Bel, thank him for our victory. My muscles relaxed with the thought of the bathhouse, I chuckled as I thought of the players at the amphitheatre and the productions I had seen, and I surged with happiness at the familiar sights.

As we walked through the streets, the people bowed to their king. He stopped frequently to bid his people thanks for their loyalty, and to report the good fortune of the army. When we reached the palace, Odenathus' escort and I followed him up the marble steps where he was met by Commander Worod, who nodded in greeting.

'My lord,' he said, 'it is good to see you return from the frontier. Palmyra has missed your presence, and your son awaits you.'

Odenathus smiled and I knew by the way the muscles around his face pulled that he could not help himself. He had been overjoyed at the news of another healthy boy. He had two now, he could ask for no more. I reflected how Julius would be pleased to hear he had a grandson, a male of his own bloodline, and felt a smile creep upon my own face.

'It is good to see you also, Worod,' Odenathus replied. 'It has been some time since our frontier held this well. We should all be celebrating this time of peace in a land that has known too much war.'

We reached the top of the steps and Odenathus gripped Worod's hand and embraced him.

'Times are good, my friend.'

'They are good indeed,' the commander replied as we stepped out of the sun and into the shade of the palace. 'However there are pressing matters we must discuss. I have reports of usurpers rising now that Emperor Valerian is captive; men who could rally the Roman armies. And ...'

'To be expected,' Odenathus replied as we strolled through the vast halls of the palace. 'And Valerian is captive no longer. He is dead.'

Worod looked surprised and stopped walking, but Odenathus continued.

'We can talk of it later. Right now, I wish to see my son.' The king flicked a hand to the escort and they fell away.

From deep in the palace I heard footfalls. A moment later Zenobia rounded a corner. She ran the length of the hall and my heart raced as I trembled at the sight of her. She stopped short of us. Her face shone and her eyes were bright with happiness. She walked up to her husband and her king and kissed his cheek and said, 'We have a boy, Odenathus.'

Behind her, a wet nurse carried a bundle in her arms. Zenobia parted the swaddling and took the baby from within. She cuddled him to her chest for a moment, then stooped down and placed him on the floor at the husband's feet, before straightening and bowing her head.

'He looks just like you, Odenathus,' she murmured.

There was a pause as we all waited for the king to accept the child as his own.

He stooped down, gripped the babe in his large hands and stood up. He kissed the boy's forehead and as he did so Zenobia's smile took on a youthful and infectious quality, her face full of energy. She was a girl again in that moment, fresh and innocent and with a mind for children.

She looked at Odenathus.

'He is strong.' The king offered his son a finger to grip and the baby took it.

'Just as his father is strong,' she replied.

'Just like his mother,' Odenathus said without taking his eyes from his son.

I could not help it, the surge of warmth, the happiness I felt that the boy had survived being delivered into the world, that I could see such joy in Zenobia once more.

'I have not really thanked you for everything you have done,' Odenathus went on. He took Zenobia's arm and led her to one side, the baby in his arms. The wet nurse, Worod and I turned away. Still I heard his hushed words.

'I confess there were times when my frustration with you was so great, I could not think of a way forward.' I thought of Rome as he spoke, and Zabbai's confession that the king had sent her there to be rid of her from the council. 'You are a woman, so I did not speak to you of military matters, and yet you have proven you understand much more than I ever thought you could. You have shown a great deal of courage. It would seem you were right to barter the emperor's life; we have victory because of it. Palmyra is safe. The Syrian and Roman armies are working together in a way I never imagined possible. You deserve credit for that.'

'It does not matter now,' Zenobia said. 'I have done as you asked of me; what is expected of me. I have given you a son.'

'You have, but you must understand something. My disappointment at not producing another child immediately was never with you, but with myself. I did not tell you how hard my previous wife tried to conceive a boy and the anxiety we both felt before Herodes was born. I never spoke with you or comforted you. I never appreciated how hard it must have been for you to bear that grief alone. I am glad that Zabdas was able to share some of it with you, but I cannot apologise enough for my absence.'

'There is no need,' Zenobia she whispered. 'We have a son now. We must show the people.'

He half-laughed as if with relief that she pursued his apology no further.

'We must! Commander, let the people know that I will name my boy to the city within the hour.'

Odenathus handed the infant back to the wet nurse, kissed Zenobia's forehead, and strolled away with Worod talking beside him.

Zenobia moved closer to me, and I to her. I realised nothing had changed in the time I had been at the frontier and she here in Palmyra in confinement. We were both the same people yet another life was being added to the family I had come to know.

'I hoped you would come with Odenathus,' she said.

'Of course I did. Why would I not?'

'I wanted you to see my son, and I know you will want to speak of my father,' she said, ignoring my question, but I did not care, I was here at last.

'He will be proud. As much as I consider him *my* father, I can never be of his blood. But I am of yours and your mother's and you have a boy now and he is of Julius' blood and I am more pleased than I can say. Have you sent word to your father?'

My excitement at the thought that he might be on his way back to Palmyra as we spoke, that perhaps he was already there, heightened.

'Zabdas?' She looked at me quizzically, then her mouth dropped slightly and her brows sank at the corners. Her eyes widened in horror.

I felt my stomach lurch and rise into my throat. I tried to swallow, but I could not. I feared what would come next. I willed the words not to leave her mouth, but they did.

'You do not know what has happened?' she said with little more than a whispered breath. 'I sent a messenger to Odenathus. Your paths must have crossed as you travelled here. Oh, Zabdas!'

She held out her arms to me and like a child I collapsed into them. And we embraced one another, her hand taking my head and pulling me close, my own calloused hands at her back, holding onto her. I could smell Julius' garden in her hair. I closed my eyes and the tears fell.

'Tell me he is not dead,' I said, barely capable of uttering the words.

'He is dead and in the Otherworld,' she whispered.

'How?' A single word but barely audible.

'Cut down by the Tanukh.'

We both sank to the floor—or perhaps I dragged her with me—and my throat ached with pain as I tried not to let emotion overcome me. I looked into Zenobia's eyes, hoping to see doubt in them, but there was only resignation. They did not fill with tears. They were hard, cold even. She should have wept. He was her father, after all, but she shed nothing. She had known before me.

My heart plunged deep into my stomach and I shook.

When I could feel nothing but emptiness, Zenobia pulled away, took my face in her hands, and said, 'Will you bind yourself to me, Zabdas, as my brother, as my whole brother, as Julius' son?'

My head dropped in acceptance. 'I will be whatever you need me to be.'

She kissed me firmly. Her lips were soft and full and determined. They were lips tinged with anger.

'I rid Syria of its overlord. I found Odenathus victory over the Persians. I secured him Roman legions. I have borne him a son. I will ask one thing of him in return: that he let me take soldiers south, to stand beside Teymour, so that one of us can avenge my father's death.'

I nodded again, cuffed my face dry and swallowed.

'No matter how long it takes,' I promised, 'I will seek revenge on the man who did this.'

Golden hair trembled down her back as she shook dice and tossed them across the marble floor where they skittered before coming to a stop. A boy of perhaps five or six years laughed as he fetched them. I hung back, not deliberately, just savouring the sight of my sweet Aurelia.

I had worried I no longer cared for her in the same way, because we had been apart for so many months, and in that time it had been Zenobia's face in my thoughts, her voice in my dreams; her presence I missed. But after seeing Zenobia with Odenathus, the son she had given him and the happiness I saw in them both, I knew it was time for me to put my feelings for Zenobia aside and move on. She was my half-sister. I could never have her to myself, could not keep her with me always, nor protect her from what I considered danger.

For long moments I simply stared at Aurelia, thinking of Julius and Zenobia's son and everything that had happened. I thought of the lives coming into this world, and all the men I had despatched to the other.

The boy looked up, his dark eyes guarded, and Aurelia turned and faced me.

'Zabdas!' she cried.

I walked and she ran and we embraced. I buried my face in the silk on her shoulder and breathed her scent deeply; clung to her desperately. I remembered all the things I loved about her. Her embrace was warm and caring and loving. Her voice was soft and understanding. She understood me and knew how to be there and to speak the words I sorely needed. Aurelia was there for me, and always would be.

She must have felt my grip tighten.

'You know about Julius?'

I squeezed her harder. For a moment I felt the same despair I had when I collapsed into Zenobia's arms, only this time I caught myself and mastered the sea of emotion that tried to take me. I felt anger and frustration and desperation. I wanted the man who had cut Julius down dead and I wanted him delivered to me in that moment.

I saw the boy squinting at me, his bottom lip protruding in sullen dislike. He threw the dice to the floor without breaking eye contact. I concentrated for a moment to drain the emotion from my features, and pulled away from Aurelia.

She took my face in her hands, just like Zenobia had.

'I am so sorry, Zabdas. I know how much you loved him.'

I made no reply. I had nothing to say; no words that would make anything better.

'I am pleased you came back with the king,' she went on, her hands moving to my chest, 'and that you are unharmed.'

There was a moment, brief and clear, where I realised it was probably Aurelia who had expressed a desire for me to return to Palmyra, and Zenobia had merely obliged.

I bunched her fingers in my hands and kissed their tips.

'I am glad that Odenathus gave me the opportunity, that I am looking at you right now. The gods know how much I have wanted to touch and hold you these long months.'

She smiled and pressed herself closer to me.

'It has been too long since I last held you.'

'I know. But I am afraid I will be leaving again soon. Zenobia and I will go south to avenge Julius' death. I want you to stay here, in the safety of these walls.'

She closed her eyes, pressed her lips together and nodded.

'I have to go.'

'I understand,' she murmured, and I knew the love of that girl again.

I kissed her forehead then glanced at the boy who hummed to himself as he tumbled the dice on the floor over and over.

'Who is he?' I asked.

Aurelia glanced over her shoulder at him. 'Sohrab. Whilst Zenobia was with child, Meskenit moved into the palace. She brought him with her.'

'Meskenit brought him?'

'That is right. He came with her.'

Something stirred inside me.

'Where are his parents?'

'His mother is dead,' she said, though her voice hid many unsaid words.

I let go of Aurelia and took a step toward him.

'Who was your mother, boy?' I asked.

His eyes flicked up at me.

'What was her name?' I persisted when no reply came.

'My mother was a slave,' the boy mumbled.

Aurelia put her hand on my arm, but I ignored the silent plea.

'Her name?' I demanded of the boy.

Aurelia's grip tightened and she spoke for him. 'Farva. His mother's name was Farva.'

I stared at him, not knowing what to think. Not really thinking anything. This was Farva's child, the slave-girl who had claimed to have fallen with child by me when I had never lain with her.

'Meskenit told me that he may be your son.' Aurelia's voice was not accusatory. It was not enquiring. It simply stated the fact.

'He is not and he could never be. I had never been with a woman before you, Aurelia. His mother is a liar.'

My words were heated and angry. That the lies Farva had told had come around to pass before me once more. That she had sullied my name for her own reasons.

Sohrab came across, clung to Aurelia and looked up at me, pouting.

'I told Meskenit I would care for him a while,' she said. 'We have no children of our own yet. And I can teach him everything I learned from Regulus. I can teach him about Rome!'

Aurelia was the woman who doted on me as I had consumed myself with everything but her. I had cared for Syria and I had cared for Julius and his daughter, but I did not think enough of Aurelia. She cared for me and loved me when I was not even there, and now she cared for a boy she believed might have been mine even when he was not.

I looked down at the little boy and saw myself; fatherless and alone. Suddenly I saw something in me that I hated: a selfish young man who could not give the very same thing he had taken so greedily when he had found a family. Julius had loved me, and I him, even though I was not of his blood. Could I love this boy as Julius had cared for me? Could I give him that which I had known?

I knelt on the cold floor in front of him and took his hands in mine. They were bruised and swollen.

'You fight with your friends?' I asked him, seeing the marks left by sticks from my own days of training.

His face softened a little and he nodded.

'Perhaps I can show you a few things that will help you beat your friends, hmm?'

He nodded again.

'Good,' I said, feeling a strange, simple pleasure. It had been easy to say those words and see the glimmer of excitement in the boy's face.

I got to my feet.

'The king is about to name his son to the people. We are expected to be there.'

The shadows on the palace steps faded as the sun hit them and the crowd was shrill and noisy. The citizens already knew of the birth of the king's second son, but they had been waiting in anticipation of Odenathus' return. It was strange, that the day should be one of celebration when I felt such heavy loss. I stood in the hallway of the palace with Zenobia and Odenathus.

'Your father was a brave man,' Odenathus said. 'I will miss my great and wise friend. I only wish that we had not quarrelled so often over the years. He will be honoured in the feasting halls of the gods. There is no doubt of that.'

Even with all that had happened, all the hatred and

resentment I had felt toward Odenathus in the past, the blame I found for him, I felt only sympathy as I saw the hurt and despair on his face when he discovered the fate of his friend.

'Of course he will be honoured,' Zenobia replied.

'He will save you a seat beside him, my Lord,' I said.

'He will save us all a seat at his table,' Odenathus replied, putting an arm about both mine and Zenobia's shoulders. 'You will want his death avenged?'

Zenobia looked up at him, as if wondering whether he could read her mind. But then anyone would have known we would desire revenge.

'I will give you whatever you require to achieve that. I will give you anything you need. I would have the head of the man who did this.'

'We would all like that,' I replied.

I left them and walked out into the bright glare of the sun and joined Aurelia at the top of the palace steps. Worod stood a little further along. The whole city waited for Odenathus and Zenobia to appear.

Aurelia's pale hair hung loose about her shoulders, her face paler still, and her pink lips formed a radiant smile. The sky was a vivid blue and there was no wind. Palace slaves threw bread to the people. A servant whispered to the commander, who in turn signalled for the horns to sound. The air became still and quiet for a moment, then the people of Palmyra burst into shouts and cheers and clapping.

The king and queen of the east emerged from the palace shadows. Zenobia held the second heir to the Palmyrene throne in her arms. Her magnificent emerald silks shimmered in the midday light and a loose gold braid at her waist betrayed the recent birth. Her hair was swept up and held atop her head with a golden crown, making her oval face more prominent. I had never seen anyone so entrancing. She had given birth to an heir, she had become a woman in every sense, and yet she smiled the very same smile I had witnessed the first time I met her; youthful and full of mischievous joy. Beside her, Odenathus could not have looked happier, despite the recent news of Julius. His broad grin was triumphant, and the way he looked at Zenobia was as if she could never do any wrong.

I felt my face sink at the sight, of the happiness of everyone gathered in the wake of loss, but I determined not to give in to it, not now, not when we had so much to celebrate on this day. Let revenge wait for another time, I thought, for I would surely have it. And let today be one of joy and laughter and celebration.

'Citizens of Palmyra, people of Tadmor,' Odenathus bellowed. 'I return once more from our frontier. We have defeated our Persian enemy in battle, and now we are pushing them back into their own lands.' He scanned the crowd. There were over 150,000 citizens in Palmyra, and most of them thronged the streets trying to catch the words of their king.

'I have sworn loyalty to Rome, but I swear loyalty to you, too, my people. I give each and every one of you my oath; that I will never tire of protecting these lands whilst there is breath in my body. I will never cease in my bid to rid Syria of invasion. I will push the enemy back into their own lands, or I will perish in the attempt.

'Today is a day of loss and of birth. As many of you know, Julius Aurelius Zabdilas, Stratego and friend to the people of Palmyra, is dead. He will not leave my heart, and I know he will never leave yours. Let him remain for all time the man he was; a man of the people.

'And yet with loss comes life. The gods show us favour. They have taken from us a great man, but they give us now his grandson, my own son, the second heir to the Palmyrene throne ...'

Odenathus took the infant from Zenobia and held him aloft for the whole city to see. Sobs and shouts of displeasure at the news of Julius turned to cheers and yelps which intensified until, after a moment, Worod signalled with his arm for silence once more. But the people were not for stopping. They shouted and hooted and whistled and lay prostrate on the ground as they thanked the gods for sending this sign and for telling us they had not abandoned our cause.

But my belief in the gods waned. I fought emotion as I thought of how Julius would never see his grandson. I pledged in that moment to keep this child safe, to protect him no matter what, to train him as I had been trained, so that he could defend himself from the cruel world that had taken his kin before he had ever laid eyes on them.

Aurelia touched my arm as my head bowed with the weight of grief and the promises I made myself and others.

Guards flanking Odenathus and Zenobia began rapping spears on their shields and the crowd fell silent. I sensed not one person drew breath as the naked child in the king's grip wriggled and blinked and his eyes darted curiously over the blanket of people. Then Odenathus said in a voice that carried:

'I give you my son. I give you Vaballathus.'

The story continues in
The Better of Two Men (Overlord III), Spring 2015

The Rise of Zenobia (Overlord I) is available in
ebook, paperback and audio.

Also by JD Smith, *Tristan and Iseult*.

Sign up at www.jdsmith-author.co.uk for notifications
of new releases and special offers.

HISTORICAL NOTE

Threatened by financial crisis, plague, invasion and rebellion, the 3rd Century AD saw the Roman Empire closer to collapse than ever before. Palmyra – known then as Tadmor – was a vital caravan city on the eastern trade route. It was taken under Roman control in the mid-first century but despite this, its people were of mixed Aramaic and Arabic stock, and the language used a form of Palmyrene: a mixture of Middle Eastern Aramaic and Greek.

According to an inscription made by Shapur in a rock at Naqsh-e-Rustam, Valerian brought with him a force of 70,000 from various parts of the Roman Empire in order to push back and reclaim those parts of Syria which had been captured by the Persians.

The year Odenathus acquired senatorial rank is uncertain and could be anywhere between 222 and 254, though his military achievements brought him the title Consularis, and in an inscription dated 258 he was styled "the Illustrious Consul our Lord". It is believed he was self-proclaimed "king".

Zenobia was born with the name Iulia (or Julia) Aurelia Zenobia, although this varies between languages, and on official documents she would use Al-Zabba, meaning "the one with long lovely hair". She claimed to be a descendant of Dido, Queen of Carthage, the King of Emesa Sampsiceramus and the Ptolemaic Greek Queen Cleopatra VII of Egypt.

Her father was Zabaii ben Selim or Iulius (Julius) Aurelius Zenobius/Zabdilas; a chieftain/stratego of Palmyra around 229. In other sources, Zabdilas is also noted as being a merchant. His participation in the battle on the Euphrates and his subsequent death are entirely fictional.

Although Zabdas features in history, there is no mention of his family tie to the Zabdilas family.

Emperor Valerian was taken captive by Shapur I, becoming the first and only Roman Emperor captured as a prisoner of war. Although there is no documentation supporting the idea that he was betrayed by either Zenobia or the Palmyrene's, an early Christian source claims he was used as a human footstool amongst other humiliations, and yet another source he was later flayed alive. His captivity and death have been debated by historians without firm conclusion.

Vaballathus was the second son born to Odenathus and first to Zenobia, although his birth is believed to have been in 257AD, rather than 260AD.

Those people mentioned above are recorded in history, as are Ballista, Zabbai, Pouja, Shapur I, Worod, and Jadhima, King of the Tanukh.

Thank you for reading a Triskele Book.

Enjoyed *The Fate of an Emperor*? Here's what you can do next.

If you loved the book and you'd like to help other readers find Triskele Books, please write a short review on the website where you bought the book. Your help in spreading the word is much appreciated and reviews make a huge difference to helping new readers find good books.

More novels from Triskele Books coming soon.
You can sign up to be notified of the next release and other news here: **www.triskelebooks.co.uk**

If you are a writer and would like more information on writing and publishing, visit www.triskelebooks.blogspot.com and www.wordswithjam.co.uk, which are packed with author and industry professional interviews, links to articles on writing, reading, libraries, the publishing industry and indie-publishing.

Connect with us:
Email admin@triskelebooks.co.uk
Twitter @triskelebooks
Facebook www.facebook.com/triskelebooks

Acknowledgements

Thanks go to: the Triskele team, Gilly, Jill, Kat and Liza, of which I am proud to be a part; to Perry for his above and beyond proofreading; my family and my friends and all the wonderful people I have met through the world of literature.

I take full responsibility for all factual errors, but for everything that is right I owe thanks to:

Farrokh, Dr Kaveh. *Sassanian Elite Cavalry*. Osprey, 1995.

Fraser, Antionia. *The Warrior Queens*. Phoenix Press, 1993.

Goldsworthy, Adrian. *The Complete Roman Army*.
Thames and Hudson, 2003.

Stoneman, Richard. *Palmyra and its Empire*.
University of Michagan, 1992.

Watson, Alaric. *Aurelian and the Third Century*.
Routledge, 1999.

The massive and incredibly helpful resource that is Wikipedia.

And the members of historum.com, which I have only just discovered, but whose members are enormously helpful and knowledgeable.

Also from Triskele Books

The Charter by Gillian Hamer
Closure by Gillian E Hamer
Complicit by Gillian E Hamer
Crimson Shore by Gillian E Hamer

Rats by JW Hicks

Behind Closed Doors by JJ Marsh
Raw Material by JJ Marsh
Tread Softly by JJ Marsh
Cold Pressed by JJ Marsh

Spirit of Lost Angels by Liza Perrat
Wolfsangel by Liza Perrat

Delerium: The Rimbaud Delusion by Barbara Scott Emmett

Tristan and Iseult by JD Smith
The Rise of Zenobia (Overlord Book I) by JD Smith
The Fate of an Emperor (Overlord Book II) by JD Smith

Gift of the Raven by Catriona Troth
Ghost Town by Catriona Troth

www.ingramcontent.com/pod-product-compliance
Lightning Source LLC
Chambersburg PA
CBHW022113040426
42450CB00006B/679

* 9 7 8 0 9 5 7 6 1 6 4 5 5 *